Parliamentary versus Presidential System of Government

Parliamentary versus Presidential System of Government

G.L. Verma

ATLANTIC
PUBLISHERS & DISTRIBUTORS (P) LTD

Published by
ATLANTIC
PUBLISHERS & DISTRIBUTORS (P) LTD
7/22, Ansari Road, Darya Ganj,
New Delhi-110002
Phones : +91-11-40775252, 23273880, 23275880, 23280451
Fax : +91-11-23285873
Web : www.atlanticbooks.com
E-mail : orders@atlanticbooks.com

Branch Office
5, Nallathambi Street, Wallajah Road,
Chennai-600002
Phones : +91-44-64611085, 32413319
E-mail : chennai@atlanticbooks.com

ISBN 978-81-269-1440-1

Printed in India at Nice Printing Press, A-33/3A, Site-IV, Industrial Area, Sahibabad, Ghaziabad, U.P.

The growth of cabinet dictatorship has to a remarkable extent, diminished the power and prestige of Parliament, robbed its proceedings of significance, made it appear that Parliament exists mainly for the purpose of maintaining or somewhat ineffectually criticizing an all good but omnipotent cabinet and transferred the main discussion of political issues from Parliament to the platform and the members.

–Ramsay Muir

It is not the strongest of the species that survives, nor the most intelligent, but the one most responsive to change.

–Charles Darwin

Contents

Preface *ix*

1. India's Constitutional Voyage 1
2. Constituent Assembly—Discussion on Form of Government 18
3. Reasons for Decline of Parliament 27
4. Dynastic Politics—Dilution of Democracy 31
5. Women's Representation Bill—An Unresolved Controversy 52
6. Electoral Malpractices, Poor Polling and Illiteracy 58
7. Multiplicity of Political Parties 83
8. Constraints in the Working of Coalition 103
9. Excessive Use of Power to Issue Ordinances 115
10. MP Area Development Scheme—Irregularities Galore 127
11. Substantial Decrease in Periods of Sessions—Bureaucracy Taking Parliament for Granted 133
12. Criminalisation of Politics—Bane Afflicting Democracy 145
13. Governor's Role in Working of Federal System 151
14. Presidential System as Panacea for Political Ills 158

15. Constitutional Provisions which would Require Revision for Switching over to Presidential System 200

16. State Funding of Elections—Some Aspects 205

17. Compulsory Voting—Its Feasibility and Implications 214

References 222

Preface

The declining trends in over six decades of working of Parliamentary system of government in our country have thrown open a debate as to whether it has lived upto the expectations of the founding fathers of the Constitution and also the people. Drawn from the system prevailing in U.K. for centuries and based upon the working of legislatures prior to Independence, Parliamentary system was considered to be the best suited for the geo-political conditions of India. However, the events that have taken place in its working during past six decades or so have belied all expectations. The trends which have crept into the system and led to its decline include dynastic politics, multiplicity of political parties, voters' apathy, poor polling, absence of single-party majority, adoption of dubious means to form the government, absence of healthy debates, pandemonium, boycott, absenteeism, lack of quorum, bypassing of Parliament, electoral malpractices and criminalization of politics. High cost of running the Parliament can be judged by the fact that it costs nearly Rs. 22,000 per minute to run the proceedings. This does not include the huge sum of more than Rs. 1,200 crore paid to the MPs annually under Local Area Development Scheme (MPLADS) and the enormous cost of about Rs. 13,000 crore for conducting elections all over the country. It is anticipated that nearly Rs. 40 crore are spent annually for obtaining information and preparing replies for Question Hour.

Membership of Lok Sabha is now fast acquiring dynastic and hereditary character. In General Elections-2009, as many as 200 constituencies witnessed contests by sons and daughters of highly placed politicians. Mohathir Mohamad, former Prime Minister of Malaysia, once said that a politician indulges in the biggest corrupt practice when he tries to promote or groom the political prospects of his progeny. A politician promoting his progeny while saddled in power and using his influence is entirely different from a politician who is merely related to another politician as just coincidence. The fact that dynastic politics has flourished in India where every politician is trying hard to see his sons or daughters occupying constitutional positions regardless of their merit or credentials is certainly a bad omen for the democratic set-up of the country. It is family affiliation and not caliber which has become the criteria now.

Elections to the 15th Lok Sabha saw the dynastic politics reaching its pinnacle when sons and daughters of almost every known politician came out as debutants to the new House. A long list of such debutants includes the progeny of politicians like Sharad Pawar, P.A. Sangma, Bhupinder Singh Hooda, P.S. Badal, Ajit Singh, Farooq Abdullah, Sheila Dikshit, Y.S. Rajasekhar Reddy, Madhav Rao Scindia, Karunanidhi, Narayan Rane, P.M. Sayeed, H.D. Devegowda, Mulayam Singh Yadav, Rajesh Pilot, Jagjivan Ram, S. Bangarappa and host of others. Some of these leaders went to the extent of arm-twisting the central leadership to secure ministerial berths for their kins. The manner in which Karunanidhi bargained for securing portfolios for his kith and kin and boycotted the formation of Cabinet and oath-taking ceremony surprised political analysts. Corridors of Parliament House and Assemblies may now witness discussions over family affiliations or matrimonial alliances rather than problems confronting the nation. Every legislator will now be viewed from his family background rather than his own contributions or any work at grass-roots level which will take a back seat. In fact, our entire polity is at a crossroad, taking transition from democracy to oligarchy, and the day is not far when politics will become the monopoly of a few families.

MPs are also fast losing their interest in Parliamentary works. Debating skills expected from a Parliamentarian are missing. Their speeches exhibit lack of prior preparation or any effective homework. There is an instance of Lok Sabha having passed the grants for ministries to the tune of over Rs. 11 lakh crore without any debate at all. With such trends persisting, Parliament cannot truly acquire a representative character.

Apprehensions over the efficacy of the British Parliamentary system in a vast country like ours were expressed by Dr. Rajendra Prasad, the President of the Constituent Assembly, himself. He was pragmatic enough to foresee how the Parliamentary system would charter its course in India in the years ahead. He had supported the idea of considering the Presidential form of government as prevailing in U.S.A. for centuries without in any manner jeopardizing the tenets of democracy. In his considered opinion it was to suit our socio-economic and political conditions. Along the same lines, Shri B.N. Rau, Constitutional Advisor to the Drafting Committee had, while addressing IAS probationers, revealed that there was a fairly strong current of feeling in favour of the American Presidential System of Government.

Speaking in Lok Sabha on 21 December 1954, Pandit Jawaharlal Nehru remarked:

> Why have we chosen Parliamentary democracy? Because we think that in the long run it produces the best result. If we come to the conclusion that it does not produce the best result, well, we change it, obviously because we want results. What are the results we are aiming at? National well-being and the happiness of the millions of our people.

M.C. Chagla, the then Education Minister and a renowned legal luminary of his time once wrote:

> The time has come when we must have a fresh look at the working of Parliamentary institutions in our country. We are pledged to democracy and we must be loyal to the democratic ideal. But America is no less democratic than Britain. What is suited to a small country with a unified society...may not be the right system for a country which is entirely different.

If we study the above prophetic words of the astute statesmen of their time in the present political scenario where the functioning of democratic institutions has come under a cloud, we cannot help but look at the whole matter in retrospect.

With a view to identifying the factors which led to the decline in our political system and to find some workable solutions to the major problems faced, a National Commission was set up by the Government of India on 22 February 2000 to review the working of the Constitution. The Commission, comprising nine members and headed by Justice M.N. Venkatachaliah, submitted its report on 31st March 2002. The report contains an elaborate analysis of the ills affecting the working of our political system and incorporates workable solutions as well.

India's heterogeneous character, its plurality and its diversity hold special significance in the working of democratic institutions. Increasing role of regional parties at the Centre and their active participation in the formation of coalition governments is a unique and unprecedented phenomenon. Their role is however guided by the regional factors which remain at the root of their survival. While Vasant Sathe in his book *Two Swords in One Scabbard* had assailed Parliamentary system, Shashi Tharoor, former Minister of State for External Affairs, in his article published in the *Times of India* of 16 December 2007 had also advocated for abolition of Parliamentary system as it has outlived its utility. Former President of India Dr. R. Venkataraman also expressed unhappiness over the declining trends in the working of Parliament. In his speech delivered at the India International Centre on 16th October 1999, he went to the extent of exploring alternatives and even suggested formation of a National Government.

The book *Parliamentary versus Presidential System of Government* is an attempt to analyse all aspects relating to the persistent trends in dynastic politics, its impact on the working of Parliamentary system and to find out whether the Presidential form of government with separation of powers can provide panacea for the political ills. Besides U.S.A., the Presidential system is already in practice in as many as 20 other countries including Brazil, Mexico, Iran, South Korea and Venezuela. The working of Presidential system in these countries forms part of this book.

It is hoped that the book, being first-ever analytical attempt on this subject, shall be useful to the students, teachers and researchers of Political Science, analysts, lawyers and legislators. Common readers will also find the book informative and inculcating.

I am thankful to my good old friend J.K. Nayyar for his valuable assistance in completing this work and to Raj Kumar for suggesting several important features which have been duly incorporated in the book. I am also thankful to Atlantic Publishers and Distributors (P) Ltd. for evincing interest in bringing out the book. Any suggestions for further improvement of the book will be welcome.

G.L. Verma

1

India's Constitutional Voyage

When wheels of Parliamentary system of government started rolling with the commencement of the Constitution in 1950, it was hardly felt that it would take not long for the country to do a re-thinking at the entire working of Constitutional framework within a short span. Expressing deep concern over unprincipled politics, Lok Sabha passed a unanimous resolution on January 8, 1967 for appointing a high level committee to consider the problems of legislators and make recommendations. A committee headed by Y.B. Chavan was formed to present an analytical report on the whole working and suggest remedial measures. The first ever move to drastically amend the Constitution came from no other political party than Congress, which at its *Kamagatamaru Session* in December 1975 circulated a document titled "A Fresh Look at our Constitution—Some Suggestions". Sardar Swaran Singh Committee was formed to re-draft the Constitution which was passed as 42nd Amendment to the Constitution. The said amendment was however, undone with the change of guard at Centre in the year 1977. Thereafter, R.S. Sarkaria Commission was set up in 1983 to examine and review the working of the existing arrangements between the Union and the States. In May 1998, the United Front Government formed Indrajit Gupta Committee to examine issues relating to electoral reforms particularly the proposal of state funding of elections. Then in 2000, the NDA Government formed a National Commission to review the working of the Constitution under the Chairmanship of Justice M.N. Venkatachaliah.

In retrospect, India's Constitutional voyage began with the formation of first 'Legislature' under the Charter Act of 1853 followed by several reforms, enactments and political milestones took place during 97 years till 1950. The Constitution which is proclaimed to be the longest written Constitution for a largest democracy in the world has been subjected to a hundred amendments within a span of little over five decades including one major surgical amendment the country witnessed in 1975. Process of evolution is a constant phenomenon and no system can be exception to this rule.

Framers of Constitution, while adopting Parliamentary system, were also well acquainted with the working of provincial governments under the Government of India Act 1935. They were also well acquainted with the working of constitutions in different countries particularly the Presidential form of government in United States of America and other countries. A large number of members of Constituent Assembly had vehemently pleaded for adopting Presidential system on the pattern of America where this system has been working successfully for two centuries. Dr. Rajendra Prasad, the President of the Constituent Assembly, had himself once expressed his doubts about the efficacy of Parliamentary system in our country. They were fully conscious of the fact that Parliamentary system may not provide stability. Cobbling up of majority and continue to govern often remain under cloak of uncertainty which affects the growth and development. Dr. B.R. Ambedkar had his own perception of the whole issue. He was of the opinion that in a Parliamentary system, Executive remains directly responsible to Parliament whereas in Presidential system, President, though elected by the people through electoral college does not have such a constant responsibility and needs no confidence of legislature to win. To him responsibility was more preferable than stability. Addressing to this core issue, he told Constituent Assembly—"The Draft Constitution in recommending the Parliamentary system of executive has preferred more responsibility to more—stability."

One of the major contributory factors which prompted framers of the Constitution to adopt Parliamentary system was the experience drawn from the legislative reforms introduced at different stages in the past. Even when the country was under the rule of East India Company, there were several attempts from British Parliament to set up Councils and legislature with limited representations to Indians. In 1857 when rule of East India Company came to an end and country came under the direct control of British Parliament, the process of legislative reforms expedited and representations of Indians were increased. For the purpose of studies of evolution of these legislative reforms we can divide the period into two parts—(1) Evolution of legislative reforms under the rule of East India Company and (2) Reforms introduced when country came under the direct rule of British Government.

Evolution of Legislative Reforms under East India Company Rule

The coming of East India Company and its acquiring of economic and political control over the country marked watershed in the history of India. While it led to several sweeping changes in every sphere of socio-economic and political life, it also paved the way for political events of enormous significance. The Company which came to India as a trading concern, soon started expanding its wings to acquire political and military hegemony. The officers of the Company indulged in worst form of inconceivable corrupt practices. The stories about their amassing huge wealth became a talk of the town in London. A member of British Parliament Sir George Cornewall Levis had to remark—"no civilized government ever existed on the face of this earth which was more corrupt, more perfidious and more rapacious than the Government of East India Company from 1756-1772." This phenomenon soon led the British Government to find out ways to clip the wings of the Company and its officers. The British Government decided to bring the Company under parliamentary control and the Regulating Act 1773 came as a step in this direction.

Regulating Act 1773

The Regulating Act 1773 was the first act through which British Parliament pricked the balloon of Company's *de facto* sovereignty over the vast territory of India. It laid down certain regulations for the company and set up a government of Bengal consisting of a Governor General and four Councillors having whole civil and military government of the Presidency of Bengal, Bihar and Orissa. Councils of Bombay and Madras were also brought under the control and subordination of the Governor General and Councils. Through an another significant provision, the power to establish a Supreme Court in Bengal with jurisdiction over Bihar and Orissa was vested with the Crown. The civil jurisdiction of the Court was expanded to cover British subjects and the employees of the East India Company. The Governor General and Council were empowered to make and issue such rules, ordinances and regulations for the good order and civil government of the said United Company's settlement at Fort William and factories and the places subordinate thereto, as shall be deemed just and reasonable and to set and impose reasonable fines and forfeiture for the breach and non-observance thereof. The provisions made in the Act were great landmark in the evolution of legislative history culminating in formation of Parliamentary system at a later stage. The condition incorporated in the Act that the Governor General and Councils shall not make rules and regulations which can be repugnant to the laws of England holds a special significance. The Governor General and Councils had to keep the laws of England in full view while making any rule or regulations. This was by far the most remarkable check on the overblown suzerainty of the company. Moreover, it was made mandatory for the Governor General to get all such rules and regulations duly registered with Supreme Court which had the power to veto the laws submitted to it for registration. Such rules and regulations even if registered, were appealable to King-in-Council in England. But the pendency of such an appeal was not allowed to hinder the coming into immediate operation of the law. Every rule or regulation framed by the Governor

General and Council was not only required to be registered but it was mandatory to forward all such regulations to England and the power was reserved to the King-in-Council to disapprove them at any time within two years.

The above provisions were however subjected to drastic change through the Amending Act of 1781 and Pitts' India Act 1784. The Governor General and his Council was made free from the jurisdiction of the Supreme Court and the strength of the Council was reduced from four to three. Nevertheless, the Governor General and Councils had, practically, vast powers in every sphere of governance whether executive, legislative and judicial. There was no separate judiciary with independence as its common feature.

Regulating Act and subsequent Act of 1781 and 1784 hold historic significance as they marked the beginning of Parliamentary control over governance of India notwithstanding the existence of enough loopholes and drawbacks prevalent in the system.

Charter Act 1833

While introducing reforms in India's political system, British Government wanted to remain steady and firm and was opposed to any hasty action. That was why it waited for coming to an end of the twenty years charter in 1833 and find an opportunity to review the working of the Company's rule. While renewing the charter of the Company for another term of twenty years, it thought in its discretion to terminate the trading rights of the Company and confining its scope to act like an administrative agency of the Crown in India. For the first time, by the Charter Act 1833, sole legislative powers in India were vested in the Governor-General in Council which consisted of the Governor-General and four ordinary members. While three members were to be appointed by the Company, the fourth had to be appointed from outside the services of the Company. The legislative powers of the Governor General in Council extended to the making of laws for all persons, places, things and courts whatever within and throughout the whole and every part of the Company's possession in India. However, this power was not to exclude British Parliament whose power was inalienable to make any law for India. For the first time, the phrase 'Government of India' was used to describe the administrative set up working under Governor General. The Act holds special significance as it set in motion a legislative history. The laws enacted prior to the coming into force of Charter Act 1833 were called 'Regulation' and not 'Acts'. But under this arrangement, the laws passed by Governor-General in Council were known as Acts.

In an another significant step, the Charter Act 1833 provided that the texts of proposed legislation should be so made known to the public as to afford opportunities to the persons or classes whom they might particularly affect to offer their comments or complaint to the legislature. Taking a cue from the British Parliamentary practice, the procedure was adopted under which every Bill had to pass through three stages of First, Second and Third Reading and publishing every Bill in the official Gazette for public information was made mandatory. However, this four-member legislature was awfully inadequate in its strength and devoid of the benefit of plurality of views. There soon emerged a strong demand for expanding the participation in the Council.

The Charter Act 1853

The expiry of twenty years charter and demand for its further extension provided yet another opportunity to the British Government to review the whole administration under Government of India headed by Governor General in Council. However, the demand for extension of charter was opposed in both India and the Britain and several petitions to this effect were sent to the British Parliament. In a major move the British Government decided to enlarge the strength of the Council from four to six members. Based on the views of concerned authorities and the people, a Charter Bill was introduced in British Parliament which was passed by both the Houses and became an Act on 20th August, 1853. The Council framed its own Rules conforming to the Parliamentary system. A rule was incorporated under which a member had to address the Chair, use courteous language in debate. A member had to address to the Chair only and not to the members. Full opportunity for discussion was afforded to the Legislative Council and to the public. Press Reporters were allowed to sit in the gallery and publish the decisions in the newspapers for the interest of the people.

The Charter Act 1853, though a milestone in the evolution of Parliamentary system in our country, it had hardly anything to enable Indians to participate in law-making process either directly or indirectly. All the six members of the Council were Britishers and no representation whatsoever was given to the Indians. By not granting any representation to Indians, the British Government enraged the people which became one of the contributory factors culminating in Revolt of 1857.

Evolution of Legislative Reforms after Revolt of 1857

The first war of Indian independence was Revolt of 1857 which the British described as "Sepoy Mutiny", transformed the entire political scene of the country. While it ended the East India Company's rule, it heralded the taking over of political reins by the British Government in the name of Crown and the Parliament. The revolt had shaken the foundation of British Government to such an extent that its ramifications were to be seen and felt for years to come. British Government was fully conscious of the fact that their first and foremost task was to win the confidence of Provinces, Rulers and the people who remained alienated due to negative policy of the East India Company rule. The Queen's Declaration and its contents speak the volume of this factual position. The vast territories which remained under the control of East India Company now came under the direct control of the British Government which ruled through Secretary of State for India and Viceroy. The revolt quickened the pace of events and gave a strong signal to the Britishers that a constant alienation of Indians would be counter-productive. In pursuance to the Queen's Declaration, British Parliament passed the Act of 1858 under which provinces were restored to their dignity and political existence.

The Government of India Act 1858 called as an 'Act for the better Government of India' was passed by British Parliament and all the territories and all the properties of the Company except its capital stock were vested in the Crown.

The military and naval forces of the Company were deemed to be the military and naval forces of Her Majesty. The Council of the Governor General of India was to consist of 15 members out of whom eight were to be appointed by the Crown and seven elected by the Directors of the Company. The Secretary of State was to be the President and the Council with power to note at its meetings. All the treaties and contracts made by the Company would be binding on the Crown. The Act had, however, limited scope. Derby told the House of Lords that it did not pretend to deal with complicated and difficult questions which will, no doubt, within the next few years, frequently engage the anxious attention of Parliament and the country.

Indian Councils Act 1861

The Act of 1861 which was in furtherance to the process of reforms as committed at the time of moving Government of India Act 1858 brought radical reforms which include enlargement of representation in the Council. It provided for setting up the post of Secretary of State for India and Viceroy to be appointed by the British Government. For the first time, Viceroy appointed three Indian Maharaja Sir Narendra Singh of Patiala, Raja Dev Narain Singh of Benares and Raja Sir Dinkar Rao Raghunath of Gwalior to the newly Constituted Legislative Council. However, it made no difference since these Rajas had sided with the British during Revolt of 1857. Subsequently, when Lord Ripon became Viceroy, he nominated several Indians having social standing such as Syed Ahmed Khan, Ras Behari Ghosh and Raja Shiva Prasad. They were however not sensitive enough to gauge people's aspirations and ventilate them in the House. The Indians hardly made any worthwhile contribution in the debates. They lacked interest as well as debating skills to leave any imprint during the discussion. The Council's powers were limited and its status was sometime described as "Debating Society". The aftermath of Revolt had in fact saw the revival of Legislative Councils in the Presidencies without much power of interference in day today working of the Government. The Act of 1861 specifically provided that the functions of the

Governor General in Council were strictly limited to legislation. It provided—"No business shall be transacted at any meeting for the purpose of making laws and regulations other than the consideration and enactment of measures introduced into the Council for the purpose of such enactment. Every law or regulation made by the Council would be subject to the assent of the Governor General he could declare that he assents to the same, or that he withholds his assent from the same, or that he reserves the same for the signification of the pleasure of Her Majesty thereon.

Indian Councils Act 1892

As the Governor General in Council had no powers relating to Financial affairs, the Viceroy Lord Dufferin sent his proposal to the Secretary of State suggesting reforms that Parliament should consider some form of election as to justify a belief that it might be safely and advantageously adopted. But this request was not acceded to. There was no mention of election in the Bill but the Council was empowered to make rules authorizing the discussion of the Annual Financial Statement and asking of questions. No member, however, had the power to propose any resolution or to divide the Council in respect of any such financial discussion or the answer to any question.

Government of India Act 1909 (Morley Minto Reforms)

It can not be disputed that cosmetic changes in Council and other legislative measures introduced earlier had hardly any impact on the teeming millions of India. The unrest which was growing among people was fuelled further by the partition of Bengal and enactment of the Official Secrets Act. Congress, had by now, taken upon itself the role of expressing people's resentment and sought for radical reforms in the legislative and administrative set up. Gopal Krishan Gokhale described the Viceroyalty of Lord Curzon by drawing parallel with the times of Aurangzeb with same policy of distrust and repression and same centralization of rule as prevailed during letter's regime. Followed by such severe criticism, certain events followed leading to the reforms in political set up. Liberals had come to the power in Britain. Morley, who was known as a philosophical radical, was appointed as Secretary of State for India. Viceroy Lord Minto was also keen to introduce some changes to meet the aspiration of Indians.

Under the Indian Councils Act 1909, the maximum number of members of the Indian Legislative Council was raised from 16 to 60 excluding executive councilors who were ex-officio members and the size of the Councils in the Presidences was also more than doubled. For the first time Councils had elected members. The membership of the Council was divided into four categories—(i) The ex-officio members who were holding certain government office, e.g. the Governor General and the members of his Executive Council, (ii) Nominated official members who were nominated from amongst the officials of the Government of India, (iii) nominated non-official members, i.e. men from public life nominated by the Government, and (iv) finally, the elected members. Out of total strength of 68 members, there were 7 ex-officio, 28 nominated officials, 5 nominated non-officials and 27 elected members. The election method for these 27 seats was not general but by classes, communities and interests. Muslims were given separate electorate. They could be elected by the other non-reserved constituencies as well. From the composition of the Council, it is clear that taking the nominated members and ex-officio members, the Britishers had a major say in the deliberation of the Council. Members of the Council were given power to move resolution on any matter of general public interest and to divide the council upon them. Resolutions seeking alteration in Budget proposal could be moved. But Government was free to accept or reject the Resolution.

While introducing reforms, Morley had himself stated, "The Imperial Supremacy shall not be compromised by any degree." Hence not much powers were conferred to the Council. Nevertheless, the members fully availed the powers, though limited, to raise questions and bring resolutions which resulted in changes in the working of the Government. Quality of speech by Indian members was improved and issues relating to public interest were highlighted in more effective manner than in the past.

The reforms introduced under Act of 1909 however sowed the seeds of communal politics in India. The grant of representation on the basis of communities was the most retrograde move fraught with dangers which ultimately paved the way for the partition of the country. Though, claiming to establish Parliamentary system, it was hardly given power to censure the government or bring adjournment motion, etc. which are normally exercised in any Parliamentary system. Morley had spoken in the House of Lords that if it could be said that this chapter of reforms led directly or necessarily up to the establishment of Parliamentary system in India, I, for one, would have nothing at all to do with it.

The Morley-Minto reforms of 1909 met with severe criticism at the hands of the critics. These were aimed to divide people by creating a wedge between two communities—Hindus and Muslims. During the operation of reforms, several anti-people laws such as Indian Press Act 1910 and Criminal Law Act 1913, etc. with stringent measures were enacted. The British Government spent over 146 million pounds from the revenues of India to meet war expenses which broke out in 1914. Lacs of Indian jawans were recruited and taken to battlefield during First World War. India was thus a banker for the British Government to finance war expenses. All these events angered the Indian leadership as well as the people and unrest became a sweeping factor throughout the country.

Government of India Act 1919 (Montague Chelmsford Reforms)

Realizing the portents of simmering discontent among Indian masses, British Government made a declaration on August 20, 1917 in the House of Commons. Making this declaration, Montague the Secretary of State, laid stress on the increasing association of Indians in every branch of administration. It promised self-government within British empire. The Declaration of August 20, 1917 proved to be a landmark in the Constitutional history of India as India would be treated like other dominions of the British Commonwealth.

In fact, the declaration came when First World War was at its peak and British Government did not want to take any risk of further antagonizing Indian people at a time when their help and assistance was the need of the hour. Moreover, the Declaration was for uncertain time. An element of indefiniteness was a great dampener on the spirit of the Indians.

The Government of India Act 1919 made drastic changes in the entire government set up. It divided the subjects into Central subjects which concerned the whole of India and provincial subjects for which Provincial governments had to make laws. Provincial subjects were further divided into two parts, viz. *Reserved subjects* and *Transferred subjects*. Subjects like Land Revenue, Irrigation, Law and Order, Industrial matters, etc. were kept as reserved subjects while the Public Health, Sanitation, Education and Agriculture, etc. were kept as Transferred subjects. This came to be known as the system of Dyarchy which worked for over a period of sixteen years but it worked creakily. Governor enjoyed a dominating position in the whole Dyarchical system and ministries had to depend upon his office for minor to major matter. The Central Legislature, was entirely remodeled on the basis of bicameralism. By adding a second chamber, i.e. Council of State to the Legislative Assembly, a sort of prelude was created for the future bicameral Parliament in India. The franchise of the Assembly was based on property qualifications and varied from province to province. So the actual working of Government of India Act 1919 was not in conformity with the letters and spirit of August 20, 1917 Declaration.

The reforms introduced under the Government of India Act 1919 proved as remedy worse than disease. The dyarchical system as introduced for Provinces collapsed due to inherent contradictions. It failed to fulfil the aspirations of the masses. Another factor was the national awakening that had scaled new heights. Whole nation was on the move for independence and struggle echoed in every town and village. Simon Commission was boycotted and people were in no mood to yield to the British tactics. It was in the backdrop of these circumstances that the British Government had to convene a 'Round Table Conference' of the representatives of the Princes and the British India at London. Based on the extensive discussion, the British Government extensively amended the Government of India Bill which received the Royal assent on August 2, 1935. With the enactment of Government of India Act 1935, the following changes in the political set up were introduced:

Division of power between centre and the provinces

For the first time, British Government reconciled to the idea of establishing a Federation of provinces. The accession of the States to the Federation was however optional and terms on which a State joined the Federation were to be set out in an *Instrument of Accession.* The Federal Legislature could make laws for the States only in relation to the matters specified in the *Instrument of Accession.* Powers were also distributed and Central Legislature was to make laws in respect of subjects pertaining to the Federation as such leaving provincial subjects to the Provincial legislatures. The residuary powers of legislation could be assigned by the Governor-General to the Provinces or the Centre. The Federal Executive was to be composed of the Governor-General and a Council of Ministers. The ministers were to be chosen and appointed by the Governor General. Subjects like external affairs, defence ecclesiastical administration and tribal areas were chosen for the ministerial control. The Governor-General had full powers to legislate in respect of a reserved subject or a special responsibility, either by a temporary ordinance or a permanent Act.

The Federal Legislature, which subsequently became the replica of our present Parliament, was to consist of the King, represented by the Governor-General and two Houses namely the Legislative Assembly consisting of 375 members. The representatives were not to be elected directly but indirectly by Provincial Assemblies, the various communities voting separately for their own representatives in accordance with the system of proportional representation with single transferable vote. The Council of States (Upper House) was to consist of 260 members out of which 104 were to represent the Indian States, 6 to be nominated by the Governor-General. The remaining members were to be directly elected by territorial communal constituencies and twenty two seats were to be set apart for smaller minorities, women and depressed classes.

The Act set up a Federal Court which was to consist of a Chief Justice and not more than six other judges. The judges were appointed by warrant under the Royal Sign Manual. A judge could be removed only by His Majesty, the King on the ground of misbehaviour and infirmity of mind or body provided a Judicial Committee makes such a recommendation.

The working of the provincial and State Governments under the Government of India Act 1935 can not be termed as satisfactory. The coming of the Congress in office was not liked by the Muslim League which started demanding the partition of the country. Muslim League in its resolution passed on March 23, 1940 at Lahore session declared that no constitutional scheme would be workable unless it is designed on the territorial re-adjustments on the basis of Muslim community residing in places predominantly.

The failure of Ministries, after-effects of World War II and fervor Nationalistic movement for independence turned the whole apple-cart and the British Government had no option but do something drastic to contain the hostilities in this sub-continent. Another development which paved the way for the independence of the country was the coming of Labour Party in power in England. Immediately on its taking over, the Labour Government in Britain announced that a Mission of three Cabinet Ministers would be sent out to India to explore the possibility of an immediate settlement of the India problem. Lord Attlee, the Labour Prime Minister, declared in the House of Commons on March 15, 1946 that it is wonder how India, which is a nation of 400 million people had sent her sons to die for the freedom during World War II, should herself fight for the freedom to decide her own destiny. He expressed the desire to help India to set up the machinery for ensuring this country to decide her own course of destiny. The three Ministers forming part of Cabinet Mission arrived at India in the same month. However, when no settlement could be reached, the decision of the Mission was announced that there should be a

Union of India, embracing both British India and the States, the Constituent Assembly shall be set up with due representation to all communities. The Cabinet Mission plan was accepted by all the parties and elections to the Constituent Assembly took place in July, 1946. The Muslim League contested the elections and could win only 73 seats while Congress 211. Realising its weak position in strength, it subsequently decided to boycott the Assembly and demanded for separate Constituent Assembly for Pakistan. The Viceroy Mountbatten issued a Statement on June 3, 1947 declaring that the partition of India and also of the Provinces of Bengal, Assam and the Punjab was the only solution for solving the political tangle. The conduct of referendum in this area was proposed by Mountbatten which was accepted by the Congress, the Muslim League and the Sikhs. The referendum was conducted and the electorate of North West Frontier Province decided in favour of Pakistan. The electors of Sylhet decided to join India. These outcome subsequently formed part of the Indian Independence Act 1947.

The India's Independence and its Fall Outs

The provisions of the Indian Independence Act 1947 proved to be the landmark of the Constitutional History of India. It formally declared the partition of the country and setting up of India and Pakistan as two separate and sovereign countries. Under this Act, each of the Dominions was to have a Governor General who was to be appointed by the King. It declared that the paramountcy of the British Crown over the Indian States was to lapse. The Constituent Assembly which was set up under the Cabinet Mission Plan was now to be considered as a sovereign body under this Act. The formation of Constituent Assembly with Congress in a dominating strength and setting up of a Provisional Government at Centre headed by Nehru left Mohd. Ali Jinnah sulking and fuming. As stated by Granville Austin, *the Constituent Assembly was a one-party body in an essentially one-party country. The Assembly was the Congress and the Congress was India. There was a third point that completed a triangle, the government for the Congress was the government too*. The Congress refusal to form a coalition was a serious error of judgment, it shattered the faith and confidence of the Muslims in the *bona fide* of the Congress. Muslims became wary of the future as their participation in the governance became totally uncertain. They argued that if the Congress could be so self-centered in the limited sphere of provincial autonomy, their interests were unlikely to be protected in the all powerful Central Government under Congress rule. Finding a setback to his ambitions, Jinnah started talking of "Direct Action" without explaining its nature and revealing as to what sort of action he had in his mind and against whom it is intended to be directed. His call of Direct Action fomented communal riots in Calcutta, Bihar and most of the part of the country which continued for several days unabated causing immense loss to the lives and property besides problems of rehabilitating the displaced persons. More than 3000 people were killed and property worth thousand of crores was destroyed in the orgy of communal violence at the hands of frenzied mob. To assuage the feelings of Jinnah and other leaders of Muslim League, Lord Wavell tried to ensure participation of Muslim League in the Interim Government. Jinnah nominated five persons to join the Interim Government. But joining of government by Muslim League was not to cooperate with but to create problems for it. A Muslim League nominee, on joining the provisional government openly declared—"We are going into the Interim Government to get a foothold to fight for our cherished goal of Pakistan."

Finding the rift between Congress and Muslim League increasing, British Government started evaluating the partition of the country as the only solution to India's vexed and volatile political problems. On February 20, 1947, Lord Attlee, the then British Prime Minister made a statement in Parliament that it was the definite intention of the British Government to affect the transfer of power to responsible Indian hands by a date not later than June 1948.

All these events plus after-effects of World War II hastened the activities leading to the partition and the independence of the country. In furtherance to the Mountbatten Plan, the Indian Independence Act 1947 was enacted under which the date of August 15, 1947 was fixed as date of independence and formal transfer of power which is to remain a great landmark event in the history of India.

The history of legislative reforms which commenced since Charter Act of 1833 and continued till the enactment of Government of India Act 1935 made Indian people aware of the working of the Parliamentary system. During this long period, they acquired a good measure of experience of the working of legislature. A large number of our political leaders were in fact the product of the working of these institutions. Aflame with nationalistic fervor and patriotic feelings, they became ardent protagonists of reform-process and by virtue of their skilled communicative expertise, they could awaken the masses who were hitherto subjected to neglect and untold miseries. It was this experience together with ardent desire to build a new India that enable our leadership to contribute to the task of framing up of the Constitution for posterity.

It can not be disputed that Government of India Act 1935 and the working experience of the governments at Provinces greatly enabled the Constituent Assembly to undertake the onerous task of laying the foundation of the Constitution. It was a treasure house of working experience which enabled framers of the Constitution to usher India into an era of peace, prosperity, liberty and fraternity under a democratic set up. Another aspect which initially caused concern to the framers of the Constitution was that the Constituent Assembly, though an elected body, was not a sovereign assembly. It was set up under Cabinet Mission Plan which on its own was not adequate to confer a sovereign status to the Constituent Assembly. It was only under the Indian Independence Act of 1947 that a power to frame the Constitution was duly and legally conferred upon the Constituent Assembly.

The Indian Independence Act 1947 was a landmark event in the history of India for not one but several reasons. It not only affirmed the independence of India but also divided India into two sovereign nations. It also provided for setting up of the Constituent Assemblies for both the newly independent countries with sovereign rights to decide the destiny of teeming millions and posterity.

2

Constituent Assembly—Discussion on Form of Government

The Constituent Assembly commenced its work on December 9, 1946 when its first session began in the Constitution Hall (now called Central Hall of Parliament House). Dr. Sachchidananda Sinha was invited by Acharya J.B. Kripalani to be the temporary Chairman of the Assembly since he was the oldest amongst all the members. Two hundred and eight members were present on the first day as all the members belonging to Muslim League chose not to attend the session. The Constituent Assembly sat for 2 years, 11 months, 19 days and held 12 sessions in all consuming 167 days. Out of 167 days, 114 were devoted to consider the Draft Constitution, prepared by the Drafting Committee. The total expenses incurred on the working of the Constituent Assembly came to somewhere around Rs. 63.96 lacs.

Unlike American Constitution which was framed by Philadelphia Convention under tight security, vigil and top secrecy, the debates of the Constituent Assembly were open and given wide coverage. The visitors galleries remained packed to their capacity. People took active and keen interests in the debates and as per record more than 53,000 visitors were admitted to the visitors gallery for viewing the members debating over Draft Constitution.

The Constituent Assembly, when it set to commence its working, had to undertake various preliminaries like framing of its own Rules of Procedure, to collect and distribute voluminous background material amongst members and also the text of the Constitution of about 60 countries classified in two broad categories namely (i) the British Commonwealth countries, viz. Australia, Canada, Ireland, Leeward Islands and South African and (ii) The constitutions of the countries such as Germany, Switzerland, USA and USSR. A background material comprising fundamental rights and system of representations adopted in different countries was also compiled for distribution among members. To obviate any hiccup at a later stage, members of the Constituent Assembly decided to form a Committee to draft the Constitution. Dr. B.N. Rau was appointed as Constitutional Advisor and was especially deputed to visit USA, Canada, Eire and Britain for personal discussions to be able to present a comprehensive and authentic report based upon the actual working of the Constitutions of different countries. The Drafting Committee took 141 days to prepare a Draft which was submitted to the President of the Assembly on February 21, 1948 for its presentation before the Constituent Assembly.

With the presentation of Draft Constitution, a clause-by-clause consideration could commence on November 15, 1948. A prolonged studies and debates led the President of the Assembly Dr. Rajendra Prasad to comment in these words—"if the people who are elected fare capable and men of character and integrity, they would be able to make the best even of a defective Constitution. A constitution, like a machine is a lifeless thing. It acquires life because of the men who control it and operate it and India needs today nothing more than a set of honest men who will have the interest of the country uppermost before them. We can only hope that the country will throw up such men in abundance." How far we have come alive to these expectations is a matter of special significance to be elucidated upon in the chapters ahead.

Members of the Constituent Assembly were well acquainted with the working of various forms of government in different countries. The Draft Constitution, however, recommended for the setting up of Parliamentary system of government notwithstanding its inherent weaknesses. Commencing debate on this issue Dr. B.R. Ambedkar told the Assembly (*Constituent Assembly Debates*, Vol. 7, p. 33)—"The Draft Constitution in recommending the Parliamentary system of executive has preferred more responsibility to more stability. A student of Constitutional law if a copy of a Constitution is placed in his hands is sure to ask two questions. Firstly, what is the form of Government that is envisaged in the Constitution and secondly what is the form of the Constitution? For these are the two crucial matters which, every Constitution has to deal with. I will begin with the first of the two questions.

In the Draft Constitution there is placed at the head of the Indian Union a functionary who is called the President of the Union. The title of this functionary reminds one of the President of the United States. But beyond identity of names there is nothing in common between the forms of Government prevalent in America and the form of Government proposed under the Draft Constitution. The American form of Government is called the Presidential system of Government. What the Draft Constitution proposes is the Parliamentary system. The two are fundamentally different.

The Presidential system of America is based upon the separation of the Executive and the Legislature so that the President and his Secretaries can not be members of the Congress. The Draft Constitution does not recognize this doctrine. The ministers under the Indian Union are members of Parliament. Only members of Parliament can become Ministers. Ministers have the same rights as other members of Parliament, namely that they can sit in Parliament, take part in debates and note in its proceedings. Both systems are of course democratic and the choice between the two is not very easy. A democratic executive must satisfy two conditions—(i) It must be a stable executive and (ii) It must be a responsible executive. Unfortunately it has not been possible so far to devise a system which can ensure both in equal degree. You can have a system which can give you more stability but less responsibility or you can have a system which gives you more responsibility but less stability. The American and the Swiss system give more stability but less responsibility. The British system on the other hand gives you more responsibility but less stability. The reason for this is obvious. The American Executive is a non-Parliamentary Executive which means that it is not dependent for its existence upon a majority in the Congress, while the British system is a Parliamentary Executive which means that it is dependent upon a majority of the members of Parliament. Under the non-Parliamentary system, such as the one that exists in the USA, the assessment of the responsibility of the Executive is periodic. It takes place once in two years. It is done by the Electorate. In England the assessment of responsibility of the Executive is both daily and periodic. The daily assessment is done by members of Parliament, through questions, Resolutions, No-Confidence Motions, Adjournment Motions and debates on addresses.

Although both the Parliamentary system of Government of Westminister type and the Presidential form of Government as existing in USA are the democratic system reflecting will of the people, the difference between the two systems is over the responsibility of the executive. In Presidential form, the executive, i.e. the President is not answerable to the legislature and he is not to depend upon the confidence of the majority of the legislature. He is an independent executive and is supposed to execute the laws passed by the legislature. Whereas Parliamentary system is marked by the unique system wherein the executive powers are vested in the Cabinet headed by the Prime Minister and is not only answerable to the legislature called Parliament but is also supposed to derive its sustenance from the Parliament. The Parliament, being a supreme legislative body has the power to overthrow the entire government through a vote of no-confidence.

A study of the debates of the Constituent Assembly would make it quite clear that there was no unanimity over acceptance of Parliamentary system. There was, indeed, a sharp difference of opinion among the members. Mr. Kazi Syed Karimuddin, a prominent member spoke vehemently against adoption of

Parliamentary system of democracy. He even moved an amendment in the Draft Constitution with the proposal that the Executive of the Union shall be non-Parliamentary in the sense that it shall not be removable before the terms of the Legislature and a member of the Cabinet may be removed at any time on impeachment before a judicial tribunal on the ground of corruption or treason. He spoke, "My submission is that the parliamentary system which is functioning in India under Govt. of India Act 1935 has miserably failed as far as the Local self-government, local boards or municipalities are concerned. All over India you must have noticed that there have been deadlocks and as the worthy leader of the Muslim League said, it does not suit the genius of the people. There will be many groups and to expect that there will be a very solid and absolute stability for the Government will be a myth. We have seen in the past that in the working of the Provincial Constitution in the provinces the opposition was neglected, ignored and sometimes punished. We have also seen that the parliamentary system which is existing at present created favouritism and nepotism in regard to those people who were supporting the Ministry. The Ministers were serving the members of the party more than the people. A minister was not a humble servant of the nation but he was a humble servant of those who were supporting him in the Cabinet and therefore I say that this scheme has not worked well in the past. What we want today is a stable Government. What we want today is a patriotic Government. What we want today is a strong Government, an impartial and unbending executive that does not bow before popular whims."

"Now it is said that the parliamentary system of Government is democratic. America is a democratic country and the Constitution that is prevailing there is also democratic. We find that there is a non-parliamentary executive and the whole administration of the country is divided into three parts, one is the judiciary, the other is the Executive and the third is the Legislature. It is impossible for the Executive to defy the policies laid down by the Legislature and there is the judiciary to defy the policies laid down by the Legislature and there is the judiciary to check the excesses of the Executive. Under the circumstances when there is communal tension everywhere and when there are disruptive forces in this country, there is no other go except to have an Executive which is non-removable by the vote of legislative."

"There is no communal question in America and in spite of that, this non-parliamentary executive has been adopted there. This is a country of different religions. This is a country of different ideologies. This is a country with different cultures. At a critical moment in the history of India when we do not want internal strife when we want a formidable Government to be a bulwark against all aggression, it is necessary that in the interim period at least there should be a non-removable executive and non-parliamentary executive. The salvation of Indian people lies in this. There will be neither any favouritism nor nepotism and I plead with the House to accept my amendment."

Constituent Assembly Debates, Vol. IV

Members of the Constituent Assembly were aware of the working of Coalition Governments under the Government of India Act 1935. They opined that a coalition government depending at the mercy of different parties preaching and practising different policies and ideologies can not deliver goods. Arguing for Presidential system of democracy on USA pattern, they took the plank of stability as a foremost concern.

Mr. Hussain Imam, while speaking in favour of Presidential form of Government spoke: "I was saying that the American system has got great advantages which are not appreciated at the moment. A few days ago I learnt that Harold Laski has written a book condemning the American system of having an irremovable executive. He has praised the British system which we are adopting. What are the facts of the British system? The fact that the executive is removable in Britain does not differ materially in the day to day administration from the irremovable character of the American system. The power of not voting supplies, which is the essential part of the Ministry's working, is vested in the Legislature so that in the British system as well as in the American system the

Legislature is absolute, though in the American Constitution there is the Presidential veto. But there again they have provided so many checks and balances that the Presidential veto can be overthrown by a two-thirds majority of the House of Representatives and the Senate. So you find that the control of the purse by the Legislature is absolute practically in parliamentary system and in the non-parliamentary executive system of America. I am, therefore, of the opinion that the non-parliamentary system by means of which the President who gets not less than 51 per cent of the votes of the entire nation is a better custodian of the nation's interests than the Prime Minister who, after all, represents only one constituency and the majority of his own party members."

"I, therefore, regard that the system whereby discretion is left to the President to nominate his own Ministers is more democratic and based on better and sounder principles than the system of copying the British model. The British system was found unequal to the task when it was worked in France where the tendencies are to have small groups and parties. They found that the British system was unsuitable. USA has a different system giving the President perfect latitude to form a Government suited to the occasion. For instance during the war President Roosevelt nominated two members to his Cabinet from the party in opposition and they were given very important portfolios. So you have the same system of coalition Government in America without any of the defects which a coalition presupposes. A coalition is composed of divergent elements, each pulling in different ways. I personally think that the American system is not a quarter as bad as has been stated. It is said that the Executive is not removable. But the fact is that the executive is more easily removable in the American system than in the British system."

"In America everyday you find one Secretary of State being turned out and another being appointed. General Marshall has just come in without any furore being made. There is no one to question the right of the President to select an Executive head for the time being."

In a Parliamentary form of government, people have no role in formation of government particularly when it is a case of coalition government. Political parties use the mandate to form a government on fulfillment of their narrow ends and ambitions. If these ends are not met, they find out excuses to topple the government. So it can not be said that parliamentary system truly and directly reflects the will of the people in so far as selection of Prime Minister, Ministers and formation of overall set up of government. People have little choice except to vote for a candidate put up by a political party and the candidate so elected has little choice except to obey the whip of the political party to which he belongs. So, virtually, it is the political party which holds its sway over political events.

Another member M.A. Beg Sahib Bahadur, while speaking against adoption of Parliamentary system spoke:

> It is no doubt true that members of the Parliament are elected and after the members are elected, the leader of the majority party is called by the Head of the State to form the Government i.e. he chooses his own ministers. **Upto the stage of the return of the members to Parliament, it is democratic. From that stage, it ceases to be democratic, for the leader of the majority party may choose anyone he pleases.** The ministers no doubt belong to the party which has been favoured by the electorate, but particular ministers are not chosen by the members of Parliament. Then, Sir, the Government is formed and it is in the saddle so long as it carries the confidence of the Parliament. But take the case of a certain section of the Parliament not being satisfied with the executive but unable to throw out the Government. The anomaly is that the electorate, the real sovereign, is not in a position to throw out the Cabinet. You will, therefore, see Sir that the parliamentary system ceases to be really democratic. **In the first place Parliament does not choose the Ministers, in the second place the electorate can not turn them out. So, really, Sir, from that stage the parliamentary democracy obtaining in England which is sought to be introduced here is not democratic.**

However, Pandit Jawahar Lal Nehru did not favour the adoption of Presidential form of Government of the American type. He spoke:

> I am not concerned with the United States of America. I am concerned with India at present and I am quite convinced in my mind that if we try to adopt that here, we shall prevent the development of any ministerial form of Government and we shall waste tremendous amount of time and energy. It is said that the American Presidential election helps the forging of unity of the country by concentrating the mind of the entire country on the Presidential election and on the conduct of those elections. One man becomes the symbol of the country. Here also he will be a symbol of the country, but I think that having that type of election for our President would be a bad thing for us.

Nehru soon developed second thought on the working of Parliamentary system. On 21st December 1954, while speaking in the Lok Sabha, he remarked: "Why have we chosen Parliamentary Democracy? Because we think that in the long run it produces the best result. If we come to the conclusion that it does not produce the best result, well, we change it, obviously because we want results. What are the results we are aiming at? National well being and the happiness of the millions of our people."

If we take into consideration the apprehensions raised by framers of the Constitution during the debates in the present times, we would have no option but to conclude that they have come all proved on the test of the time. None of them could have imagined that exactly twenty-five years after the coming into force of the Constitution, it would be trampled upon on the stroke of the night of 25th June 1975 when all the democratic rights were suspended.

3

Reasons for Decline of Parliament

The question as to whether Parliamentary system of democracy has lived upto the expectations of founding fathers of the Constitution as also those of millions of people has been penetrating the minds of Constitutional experts, legislators, academicians and intellectuals since long. A lot of debate had taken place in Parliament, in Press and in Public. The outcome of the General Elections in 1967 resulting in formation of non-Congress coalition governments in several states marked the beginning of the new chapter in the working of Parliamentary democracy in India. Subsequent events replete with political stalemates and instability gave further impetus to the debate over effectiveness of parliamentary system. The Constitutional provisions relating to the imposition of President's rule under Article 356, role of Governor as political agent of ruling party at centre, attempts to topple coalition governments through defections, use of money and muscle power and other malpractices came under scathing attack. Signs of chinks in the political system and erosion of democratic norms started becoming more and more visible with alarming proportion. The matter acquired such a serious magnitude that voices of concern echoed at almost every forum including Parliament. Lok Sabha took a serious view of the whole system slipping out of hands and after a prolonged discussion passed a unanimous resolution on 8 December 1967 setting up a High Level Committee to consider the issue threadbare and make recommendations so as to salvage the democratic system from the mess-like situation into which it had fallen.

Pursuant to the resolution passed by Parliament, a Committee headed by Y.B. Chavan, the then Home Minister was formed to analyze all issues relating to the working of Constitutional set up. It gave its report suggesting various changes in the Constitutions. Political expediency and lack of will to introduce reforms, however, did not let the report to go through the process of implementation. Even while the report of Y.B. Chavan Committee was available, the Government did not consider it fit to introduce the same in Parliament to elicit opinions from all quarters. On the contrary, it chose to appoint another Committee headed by Sardar Swaran Singh in year 1975. When this Committee was set up, the country was reeling under emergency and all democratic rights of the people to freely air their views were under suspension. The political climate was not congenial to expect a free, fair and frank debate on such a sensitive matter. Nevertheless, the Government had its ways and introduced 42nd Amendment Bill to the Constitution in the Parliament. With no opposition from any quarter the Bill went through and received Presidential assent also to come on the Statute Book. The whole country was in the grip of fear. Those who swore to protect and defend the Constitution either went underground or changed their allegiances. The three years' painstaking work of the founding fathers of the Constitution was thus eclipsed at the stroke of midnight hour. The *vires* of this Amendment Bill were not to withstand the judicial scrutiny.

Thereafter, a breather came in the history of the working of the Constitution of India when in year 1977 the 42nd Amendment was undone and Constitution was restored to its past glory with greater safeguards for protection of democratic rights. However, irritants continue to haunt the working of the Constitution. Cries for electoral reforms were at their peak. A spate of suggestions and recommendations came pouring in from Committees, Institutes, political parties and Constitutional experts. Indrajit Gupta Committee and Dr. Karan Singh Committee may be named which contributed in providing some prescriptions to cure the whole system.

In sequel to the aforesaid moves initiated in the past, the Government of India vide its Resolution dated 22 February 2000 resolved to constitute the *National Commission to Review the Working of the Constitution* to make suitable recommendations. On 23 February 2000, the President of India appointed Justice M.N. Venkatachaliah, former Chief Justice of India as the Chairperson of the Commission comprising 10 other members namely Sh. B.P. Jeevan Reddy, Chairman Law Commission of India, Justice R.S. Sarkaria, former judge, Supreme Court of India, Justice K. Punnayya, former judge Andhra Pradesh High Court, Shri P.A. Sangma, former Speaker Lok Sabha, Shri K. Parasaran, Senior Advocate and former Attorney General of India, Dr. Subhash C. Kashyap, former Secretary General Lok Sabha, Shri C.R. Irani, Chief Editor and Managing Director. The Statesman, Dr. Abid Hussain, former Ambassador of India in the USA and Smt. Sumitra G. Kulkarni, former MP (Rajya Sabha). Thus the entire composition of the Commission was absolutely non-political and comprised eminent and impartial persons. Congress party, which had earlier set up Swaran Singh Committee comprising political persons, vehemently opposed the setting of the Commission and even questioned its *bona fide* with the charge of undoing the Constitution. The Commission submitted its report in four volumes to the Prime Minister on 31st March 2002. It made several recommendations to bring about reforms in electoral system. However, no debate whatsoever had taken place over those recommendations which have been lying in a state of dormancy since then. Idea never dies and in the course of any discussion for constitutional or political reforms, these recommendations will come for a scrutiny.

Fact remains that our parliamentary system of government is on the decline. Factors like dynastic politics, poor quality of debates, substantial decrease in period of Parliament session, electoral malpractices, multiplicity of political parties, horse-trading of legislators for cobbling up the majority to somehow form government have eroded the faith of people in the system. News of voters' en-mass boycott of polls as mark of protest in some of the areas have hit the headlines. They have started raising question on the utility of the whole exercise. Added to these woes is the total lack of will to introduce reformative measures. It is the political expediency rather than political probity or accountability which has come to the center-stage.

4

Dynastic Politics—Dilution of Democracy

The fast emerging trend amongst politicians to nominate their progeny as successors to their political legacy has come to stay as biggest bane of our Parliamentary system. The general elections to Lok Sabha in year 2004 brought to surface a unique factor at an unprecedented scale in which every politician was seen joining the scramble to install his or her son or daughter in politics. The practice of promoting political prospects of sons and daughters reached its crescendo in year 2009 General Elections when every politician belonging to every political party was seen lobbying for his kiths and kins. Nearly one-third of the members of 15th Lok Sabha are drawn from politicians families. Even Finance Minister Mr. Pranab Mukherjee, while speaking before H.T. Leadership Summit, supported this practice when he remarked that the practice of dynastic politics is not unique to India. He said that in countries like UK and USA too the practice is not uncommon as nearly 6 US Presidents and 56 British Prime Ministers were related to each other. He however, failed to distinguish that mere relationship by co-incidence is entirely different from a politician using his own position to promote or groom the political prospects of his progeny. He tried to camouflage the fact that dynastic politics is entirely different as it is referred to in the context of use of official position or personal influence to foster political career of family members. When a Minister or a Chief Minister works tirelessly using his status and entire resources at his command to see his family member as MLA,

MP or Minister, how far he will be able to look after the interests of people properly for whom he took oath before entering into office. This is the big question haunting constitutional analysts. General Elections 2009 saw a father-in-law joining union cabinet with his son-in-law as union ministers after having installed his son as Chief Minister of Jammu & Kashmir. Nearly 200 politicians were seen lobbying for their family members to lay their feet on the portals of Parliament. Such an unabashed flaunting of self-centered political ambitions were never seen or justified before. As more and more sons, daughters, grandchildren, nephews and nieces will enter into electoral arena, constituencies will turn into Estates and Central Hall of Parliament as better place for royal collaborations. It is genealogy overtaking ideology and oligarchy perverting democracy.

Exponents of dynastic politics argue that if son of a doctor or a lawyer can join his father's profession, what is wrong if son of a politician joins steps into shoes of his father. This argument is not compatible with Parliamentary system and principles it exhibits because Parliament and State Legislature are noble legislative institutions for serving the people and the country and not akin to doctors' clinics or lawyers' chambers. These pious institutions reposing trust of the people and the Constitution are at a higher pedestal and can not be converted into Stock Exchange or Doctors' nursing homes to earn money. They are certainly not meant for contracting business or enterprising any trade of profession. If this fallacious argument is given credence than these exponents would even justify charging 'consultation fee' for asking questions or charges for raising issue in Parliament. Similarly, there would be nothing improper if an MP or MLA charges some amount for supporting any political party to form government for the simple reason that it is his profession after all. Then there would be nothing wrong if in our judicial system also, judges too start lobbying for their progeny to step into their shoes in the same open and unabashed manner. It is pathetic and unfortunate that even media is giving credence to such arguments which can lead our constitutional system and democracy to the brink of disaster.

The factors which are attributable for thriving of dynastic politics include absence of democratic norms within political parties. There are no elections for the party posts and power of "nominations" of leaders or heir-apparent vests with the party Supremo. It is not the merit or performance but outward appearance and family affiliations which carry conviction in our political system. It is loyalty which is to be rewarded and not the merit. Once a leader chooses his son as heir-apparent, sycophants and self-seekers start rallying behind him for the reason that their survival in politics becomes dependent upon such a successor. Huge financial resources fall into the hands of leader to play with at his sweet will. This concentration of finance coupled with unlimited powers to nominate party functionaries comes as springboard to play the dice in which task of grooming heir-apparent becomes easier. There is no law to regulate internal affairs of a political party and Election Commission can not de-recognise it on any such ground. Knowing that large number of these heir-apparents are new entrants at a younger age, Congress party has coined the slogan of "young blood" which is in reality the "genetic blood". When its leaders promote dynastic politics by using the phrase "infuse young blood" in legislatures they also mean the "gene" and not ordinary blood. What can be more blatant and unprincipled defence of genealogy over ideology.

Another factor which vastly contribute to the flourishing dynastic politics is the rhetoric amongst the voters to be carried away by sympathy towards family members of politicians. It was sympathy wave towards Rajiv Gandhi which converted into votes when elections were held immediately after the demise of Mrs. Indira Gandhi. Congress has always exploited this voting behaviour to garner maximum seats in Parliament and state legislatures. Members of Parliament like Sachin Pilot, Jyotiraditya Scindia, Priya Dutt and several others got this advantage of sympathy to a larger extent. Voters like charisma and view the candidates from their rich family background. Their mindset still has the traces of feudalistic approach to the political scenario. A maxim goes which says—in monarchy it is as the king so the people while in democracy it is as the people so the ruler. Since vast multitude of our voters are not enlightened enough to see through the reality, the dynastic politics may continue to cripple and corrupt our polity. It is a state of transition from Republican Democracy to Republican dynasty. Very often, choice left before the people is limited. A limited choice of candidates before people is another factor which can not be lost sight off. If the two rival candidates are coming from their families' political legacy, they have no other option but to choose either of the two. There is no mechanism under which people can choose their alternative candidate and give him a chance to contest. So apart from factors of rhetoric, sympathy and use of money and muscle power, absence of choice comes as an additional factor which creates a compulsion for the voters to vote for candidate drawn from family with political legacy.

When 14th Lok Sabha was formed, entire media turned its focus to the first timer young guys who had became members of Parliament with the blessings of their families' political legacy. It was reported that these guys would infuse new meaning to the Parliament proceedings and would enliven debates with more pungencies. Great expectations were made that they would truly represent the younger generation of the country. They were segregated with special attribute as "young turks". However, it took not much time for anybody to realize that this was nothing but a mirage. Parliamentary Research Service has compiled the details and presented a grim picture of the performance put in by these young turk MPs in terms of attendance as well as participation in proceedings. MPs below 40, labeled as young turks had the lowest attendance record in the House. Some of the MPs could not frame questions and raise burning issues at all. Parliamentary work is in fact a tribute to the nation and its myriad problems. A novice in the field of law, finance, administration, parliamentary procedure and working of the Constitution, can hardly contribute to the debates leaving aside the daunting task of putting the bureaucracy in the dock. By contrast relatively geriatric members in 61-70 age bracket had the best attendance record in both houses of Parliament. Young MPs not only made fewer appearance in two houses of Parliament, they also found not to be upto the mark in terms of participation in the proceedings. This PRS study is sure to come as a huge disappointment for all those who have been clamouring for the induction of fresh faces in Parliament. They neither improved their attendance nor showed any skills in participation in proceedings. Their speeches were lackluster and did not enthuse the audience leave aside provoking any thought process. Lok Sabha records reveal that 18 of the 26 young MPs within age group of 25-35 years did not ask a single question during entire 14th Lok Sabha.

The role of dynastic politics does not come to an end with the election of sons and daughters to the Parliament of state legislature. It continues to show its significance in the formation of cabinet and then again when portfolios are distributed. Vir Sanghvi in his article "Politics of inheritance" *The Hindustan Times* wrote, "Family-dominated politics is a closed shop. Entry is open only to those with the right credentials of birth. Outsiders are banned from entering. And slowly but surely, true democracy is replaced by a kind of feudalism in which the peasants are given the right to choose between various aristocrats. The peasants can never enter the ruling class because the wrong blood flows in their veins." If we look at the present union cabinet, we are bound to be perplexed that almost every minister has to pay gratitude to his family's political legacy for the position he has secured. While Dayanidhi Maran is the son of Murasoli Maran and close relative of M. Karunanidhi, Kumari Selja is the daughter of former Union Minister Chaudhary Dalbir Singh, G.K. Vasan is the son of G.K. Moopanar, M.K. Azhagiri is the son of M. Karunanidhi, Parneet Kaur is the wife of former Punjab Chief Minister Amarinder Singh, Ajay Maken is the nephew of late Lalit Maken. Bharat Sinh Solanki is the son of former External Affairs Minister Madhavsinh Solanki. D. Purandeshwari is the daughter of N.T. Rama Rao. List does not end here as Tushar Chaudhary is the son of the former Gujarat Chief Minister Amarsingh Chaudhary. Jyotiraditya Scindia is the son of

Madhavrao Scindia. Sachin Pilot is the son of Rajesh Pilot. Jitin Prasad is the son of Jitendra Prasad. R.P.N. Singh is the son of former Union Minister C.P.N. Singh. Prateek Patil is the son of former Union Minister C.P.N. Singh. Prateek Patil is the grandson of former Maharashtra Chief Minister Vasantdada Patil. Agatha Sangama is the daughter of former Lok Sabha Speaker P.A. Sangama. D. Napoleon is the nephew of former state Minister K.N. Nehru, who made him his personal assistant.

In fact it is the Congress party which started with the practice of dynastic politics. It first began with Jawaharlal Nehru and continued to descend on his daughter Indira Gandhi, Sanjay Gandhi, then Rajiv Gandhi, Sonia Gandhi, Maneka Gandhi, Rahul Gandhi, Varun Gandhi and nobody can deny that other members of Gandhi clan might be nursing political ambitions to enter into the foray at an opportune given time. During his lifetime, Jawahar Lal Nehru groomed the political prospects of Smt. Indira Gandhi and nurtured the same assiduously. He had accompanied her on visits abroad and her exposure to the country and the world was done in a calculated manner. She was elevated as Congress President also. However, towering personality of Nehru did not let anybody to question his laying the foundation stone of dynastic politics. His successor Lal Bahadur Shastri did nothing to suggest that he ever intended or tried to brighten the political prospects of his sons. His short stint as Prime Minister was engrossed in tackling food shortage and war with Pakistan.

In order to promote political hegemony of Nehru family, every conceivable measure was adopted. This included clipping of wings of every senior leader who by virtue of his hold over men and matters, may pose a threat to the march of dynastic chariot. In year 1963, Kamraj Plan was adopted under which all senior leaders were to leave office and work at grass roots level. K. Kamraj, then Chief Minister of Madras (Tamilnadu) and President of Congress, proposed that prominent leaders should leave office and should go to the people. His plan was considered at the Working Committee wherein a resolution was passed authorizing Nehru to decide as to whose services were to be utilized in the government and whose in the organization and setting up a Committee to work out a detailed plan as to how the services of those who relinquished government office were to be utilized for the best advantage of the party and the country. Outwardly, the Plan was to reinvigorate the party but the move to thrust dynasty was hidden. Jawahar Lal Nehru once publicly said "I am certainly not grooming Indira for anything of the sort. That does not mean she should not be called to occupy any position of responsibility after me." However, the fact remains that she was very much "called to occupy a position of responsibility" during his own lifetime when Indira became Congress President in 1959. At a Congress Working Committee meeting, Lal Bahadur Shastri suggested the name of Indira to become the President. Gobind Ballabh Pant, unaware of the background of the move, was surprised and said "But Indira is not keeping good health. She must first...." Before he could complete the sentence, Nehru agitatedly interrupted to say, "There is nothing wrong with Indira's health. She will be better once she has work to keep herself busy." This was further confirmed when Shastri was asked whom Nehru wanted to succeed him, he unhesitatingly replied, "*His daughter*". When Nehru suffered stroke in year 1964, Kamraj suggested the name of Shastri to assist him, he asked about Indira also. "No not yet Indira, probably later" replied Nehru. Conscious about her popularity, Nehru never openly canvassed for his daughter. He told Norman Cousins "This business of picking an individual successor is something I find quite alien to my way of thinking. I am not trying to start a dynasty." He told R.K. Karanjia of Blitz—"All this talk of India in the matter of succession is totally absurd and quite unlike my native. Even if I desired to make way for Indira, do you think I have the power to force my choice on the people of India."

Once Henry Kissinger remarked: "Power is the greatest aphrodisiac". The rule has universal application. According to a Persian proverb, "When the ruler of a country takes a pinch of salt without paying its price, his officers loot the whole country." In fact corruption has many colours and overtones. Promoting son or daughter to firm up her roots in politics is the worst form of political corruption, perhaps, worse than the corruption involving mere exchange of money. In fact it was preaching of Gandhian principles and practising of Machiavellian tactics which dominated the beginning stage of country's politics. It was ideal politik but in real politik, it only boosted the forces rallying round the Nehru family to brighten the prospects of its members. While sycophants and yesmen were allowed to hold their sway, men of caliber and self-respect were grossly neglected. Loyalty and not the integrity came as a rule to roost the affairs of the party. Leaders like Morarji Desai, Chandrashekhar, S.K. Patil, H.N. Bahuguna and C.B. Gupta and others were shown the doors not because they did anything wrong to the party but because their growing influence over the party and the people could hinder or eclipse the rise of son from Nehru family. In later years, attempt to marginalize senior leaders gained momentum when Mrs. Gandhi as Prime Minister divested Morarji Desai of the Finance portfolio and herself assumed its charge. Desai resigned from the Cabinet. The Congress President Nijalingappa gave to the Prime Minister an ultimatum to restore the portfolio to Desai. Kamraj too joined the chorus, but Mrs. Gandhi remained adamant.

The dynasty, though started during Nehru's lifetime, came to prominence only in November 1975 when at the height of emergency, Indira Gandhi made it clear that her younger son Sanjay would succeed her. At this stage Sanjay was less than 30, he had no education or political experience to speak of. In fact Congress no longer remained a political party but transformed into a family firm. The year 1975 saw the rise of dynasty in its full manifestation when, Indira Gandhi making her intentions clear, authorized her son Sanjay Gandhi for drafting the political charter for the country. His Four-Point programme was to be implemented by all the government agencies. Though himself not occupying any government office, his writ prevailed over every bureaucrat, howsoever big or influential he might be. He was neither educated nor had any experience in any field, yet his words had the powerful impact. His ruthless implementation of family planning programme had earned him and his party a shock reversal in 1977 General Elections. His untimely death in an air mishap, left Mrs. Gandhi deeply perturbed. She was not to be the same again. All eyes in the Congress, than fell on her elder son Rajiv Gandhi. His lack of interest in politics at initial stage, however, dissuaded him from entering into politics. But a persistent persuasion prevailed. Temptations were hard to resist. When Mrs. Gandhi fell to the assassins, he was sworn in as Prime Minister. His assumption to the post of Prime Minister without even bare minimum experience of administration or Parliament came as a surprise to the nation. With the new son-rise on political horizon, the country's top Constitutional post of Prime Minister went as a matter of legacy. The gruesome killing of Mrs. Gandhi on the edge of General Elections 1984 transformed the wave of sympathy in electoral fortunes providing further fillip to the perpetuation of dynastic rule.

The absence of any legal or Constitutional provision to discourage dynasty has also helped it fomenting into a new phenomenon. On one occasion Madhu Limaye, a Socialist leader and a Parliamentarian, suggested that no politician who had a son or daughter ought to be allowed to become Prime Minister. In fact, it is for the political parties themselves to nip in bud such tendencies of their political leaders. Congress being a national party claiming the legacy of Gandhi and Patel should have launched a tirade against leaders nursing such ambitions. Unfortunately, it is the Congress which has commenced this game of turning political institutions into family affairs.

In the 82nd AICC plenary session held at Hyderabad in January 2006 all the national issues confronting nation and the people took back seat when Congress leaders made a beeline to join the chorus of Ra-Ra Rahul. Entire Hyderabad and its vicinity was splashed with posters projecting Rahul and Priyanka as successors to dominate the future political scene of the country. The arrival of Rahul was greeted by heart-rending slogans by Congress brigades. Not to remain behind, all senior leaders gave standing ovations. For hours it appeared that Congress had no other topic on its agenda except to declare him heir-apparent to succeed to Nehru legacy. Initially, Priyanka was also to join the session. But her attending the session was later postponed to avoid split in the glamour being assiduously built around her brother. Gurudas Kamat, leaving aside all burning issues, demanded to make Rahul member of the Congress Working Committee. "We want a reformist, accomplished, honest, upcoming leader" screamed banners hanged at every nook and corner of the city. The fact that Congressmen see the revival of their fortunes in such rhetoric exercise became more evident once again. Nobody was seen interested in knowing the agenda. All news channels were busy telecasting the minute details of the session. Brushing aside all professional ethics of journalism, reporters were focusing on details like who was wearing what and who was eating what. When a report from a TV Channel asked a Congress leader as to what qualities or contributions Rahul Gandhi possessed to qualify such a coronation-like bandwagon, he openly referred to Nehru legacy and continued what was wrong in it? While reporting the event, the *Times of India* described the session as a "Launchpad for Rahul into big league". It reported that Congressmen can't wait for son-rise and Hyderabad session was used only to induct another scion into the galaxy of leaders drawn from the family. In an editorial "Family Business" (the *Times of India*) politics was castigated as "family business" like any other business wherein ownership passes from father to son.

This trail continued when Ashok Chavan son of S.B. Chavan was proposed as Chief Minister of Maharashtra. M. Karunanidhi has by far the second largest political aspirants' family after Nehru family. He has a long list to include his sons M.K. Stalin, M.K. Azhagiri, Kanimozhi, Murasoli Maran, Dayanidhi Maran and all other members are nurturing big ambitions waiting only for the opportunity to strike. Delhi Chief Minister Sheila Dikshit has already secured a Parliamentary seat for her son Sandeep Dikshit. Then H.D. Devegowda's family is not lagging behind and his sons H.D.

Revanna and H.D. Kumaraswamy have already shown their laurels in Karnataka which resulted in handing over the baton of state to BJP. Vijayraje Scindia has its own family to include Madhav Rao Scindia, Vasundhara Raje Scindia, Yashodhara Raje, Jyotiraditya and Dushyant Singh. In Haryana, every Lal has the family as a political party itself. Devi Lal has O.P. Chautala, Abhay Chautala. Bhajan Lal has Kuldeep Bishnoi and Bhupinder Singh has Deependra Hooda. In UP, Mulayam Singh is not content by just elevating Akhilash to Lok Sabha. He put up his daughter-in-law Dimpal Yadav in the bye-election for Lok Sabha from Farrukhabad seat. Likewise, Rajesh Pilot, Biju Patnaik and S. Bangarappa have Sachin Pilot, Naveen Patnaik and Vasant Bangarappa. Sharad Pawar has already nominated his daughter Supriya Sule and got her elected to Lok Sabha. Ajit Singh and Omar Abdullah are representing Chaudhary Charan Singh and Sheikh Abdullah respectively.

In November 2008, Margaret Alva, a senior Congress leader charged that Congress seats for the elections were up for bidding as opposed to a meritocratic appointment to run for office. She had questioned the distribution of tickets to sons and daughters of about two dozen leaders for elections to assemblies of Madhya Pradesh, Chhattishgarh, Rajasthan and J. & K. in 2008, though she had herself sought a ticket for her son Nivedith. Democracy in political parties is non-existent in India. You can not enter unless you are well connected or hail from a family with political background. The party responded to the dropping her as General Secretary of the party, the Congress Working Committee and stripped of her charge of party in Maharashtra, Punjab, Haryana and Mizoram. She was accused of indiscipline on the ground that she had gone public with her allegation that party nominations were sold during Karnataka polls. She had to pay heavy price for raising voice against stinking system. Unmindful of the criticism from its own leaders, Congress continued its policy of promoting dynastic politics in elections to assemblies of Maharashtra, Haryana and Arunachal Pradesh. Constituencies turned into "families pocket boroughs". Vilasrao Deshmukh's son Amit is now MLA. Sushil Kumar Shinde's daughter Parniti Shinde also romped home as winner. NCP leader Chhagan Bhujbal's son Pankaj Bhujbal also elected. Pratibha Patil's son Rajendra Singh alias Raosaheb Shekhawat also got elected. Legacy trend in the opposition alliance also tasted some success when BJP leader Gopinath Munde's daughter Pankaja Palve also won.

The question whether dynastic politics falls within the definition of "political corruption" has now assumed significant proportion. The most widely used definition of corruption is the World Bank's working definition of corruption as "abuse of public power for private benefit" has gained acceptance. A well-known Study Group "Transparency International" (T.I.) takes a somewhat broader approach and defines political corruption as the "abuse of entrusted power for private gain". Another definition says that political corruption takes place when rulers or ruling elites misuse the resources they control for the benefit of preserving their political power for themselves and their families. Incumbents can use many techniques to maintain power of which many are perfectly legal while other are illegal and corrupt. The corrupt use of political power preservation and extension may take the form of buying political support through favouritism, clientelism, co-optation, patronage politics and vote buying. The means include the distribution of financial and material benefits money, gifts and rents but also symbolic values like status and "inclusion".

It is "misuse of political power" for whatever purpose which falls within the ambit of political corruption even if there is no exchange of pay-offs. For instance, the Watergate scandal revealed misuse of political power by the President and his office in order to undermine his opponents. Here it was misuse of political power and did not involve pay-offs for private gain. Yet Watergate scandal was viewed as political corruption because of "misuse of political power" and culminated in impeachment proceedings and ouster of President Nixon. Political corruption as misuse of political power acquires more aggravated form when indulged in to promote sons or daughters in unabashed manner. As abuse of political offices is encompassing all barriers, Iraqi Prime Minister Nuri-al-Maliki in his address to Nation on 16th Jan 2009 described "political corruption" as more dangerous and more tiresome to the State than financial fraud because it undermines the foundation of national unity. He added that the state can survive with fraudsters misappropriating public funds but political corruption undermines the entire state structure and threatens its social fabric.

Once Malaysian President Dr. Mahathir Mohamad, expressing his deep anguish over growing dynastic tendencies in politics, asked countrymen—How on earth can you curb money politics and corruption if political powers and development projects are promised to party loyalists and progeny of leaders? To curb growing corruption, he advocated for giving right to every Malaysian citizen to know the financial assets of any minister, secretaries, councilors, civil servants and judges. It needs awareness among people to regard the induction of sons and daughters into politics by politicians as corrupt practice. He said that a politician indulges in biggest corrupt practice when he promotes his progeny to acquire a niche in politics. According to Alfred McCoy, author of the best selling book *Anarchy of Families*—"the inevitable effects of political dynasties solely dominating in any political arena are dangerous and alarming. It is in this situation that the ruling elite and traditional politician are under the impression that public office is a safe and convenient haven for fame, fortune and perpetual political power. Corollary to this, the primacy of political dynasties also encourage nepotism and favouritism norms in government and of course corruption in public office, further buttressing popular disenchantment with it. The primacy of kinship ties has also resulted in individual conservatism in economic decision-making. Emphasis is put on preserving family wealth and status rather parlaying it into productive activities with consequent risks. Needless to say, that under the present set up what we have is monarchical type of government, where public officials are chosen not by sovereign people but by virtue of inheritance. If we allow this to continue then be prepared to witness the death of democracy before our own eyes. True, we do not really value our rights and freedom until we are deprived of it."

While several countries in the world are struggling against the emergence of dynastic politics, at least two countries namely Philippines and Brazil have made provisions in their Constitutions to curb the same. The evils spawned by political dynasties are so firmly entrenched that the problems remain unresolved and continue to persist in Philippine politics despite constitutional provisions. The worst part is the affluent and powerful politicians do not confine political power within themselves but it enables them to appoint or designates relatives and cohorts to various positions in the government. It is not the competence but loyalty to master which will suffice. Constitution of Philippines prohibits political dynasties under Article II(26) which lays down—"The State shall guarantee equal access to opportunities for public services and prohibit political dynasties as may be defined by law". The crux of the problem with Philippine's dynastic political system is that the Constitution of 1987 failed to define the law to implement the prohibition of political dynasty. It left out the construction of enabling law on how to implement the prohibition of political dynasty. It is highly unlikely that Philippine Congress will pass a law prohibiting political dynasty. Political clans/families have been walking all over the Philippine Senate, Congress, local and natural public offices. Grandparents, fathers, mothers and siblings are all taking turns on different seats of power all over the archipelago. Every building, project or school and even waiting sheds are named after the siblings of ruling families. Reason for perpetuation of such a worst form of dynastic politics in Philippine is not far to seek as there is no choice left with the electorate. When every candidate belongs to some ruling clan or political family, it becomes a Hobson's choice and the system is developed with all such cobwebs that no person other than a person coming from a political family can think of entering into electoral fray. Country has to undertake a long journey to curb the dynastic politics—a breeding ground for corruption which has penetrated deep into its system.

Constitution of Brazil provides another example how it provides measures to curb dynastic politics. Article 5 (Sub-Section 5) provides—"For the elections to be held on 15th November 1988, except for those who already hold an elective office, the spouse and relative by blood or marriage or relatives by adoption of the President of Republic, of a State Governor, of the Governor of the Federal District and of a Mayor who have served more than half of their term of office, are ineligible for any office within the jurisdiction of the office holder. Such safeguarding provisions were made to prevent political institutions from becoming domain of few families or attempts to monopolise them through devious means. Apart from prohibiting persons who are spouse and relative by blood or marriage or relatives by adoption, provisions have been made to debar a person from getting re-elected more than twice. US and Argentinean Constitutions too provide that a person can be President for two consecutive terms only. He can at the most get re-elected only once. Thus the chance of perpetuating power in one hands for indefinite period have been thwarted. One wonders why such provisions could not be incorporated in our Constitution. Debates of Constituent Assembly do not appear to focus much on these aspects as entire discussion was mainly covered by Westminster type of parliamentary form of government on British pattern.

There are several countries fighting against the menace of dynastic politics and these include Bangladesh, Iraq, Philippines, Pakistan, and several African countries. Neighboring countries like Nepal have already seen the bitterest consequences of dynastic politics when entire royal family was wiped out in the domestic feud. Sri Lanka is also now struggling to find some grounds of acceptability to cope with the situation. In fact, wherever families have ruled on dynastic basis, political system has remained clouded by suspense, strife and dissensions. It has led to the concentration of wealth, resources and powers with few persons close to the ruling family and has promoted sycophancy with a corrupt and demoralized administrative set up. In Bangladesh caretaker government is working hard to root out all support base for dynastic rule in the country. In its zeal to contain corruption and introduce political electoral reforms, caretaker government backed by military decided to create situation which might force the leaders of two political dynasties Khaleda Zia and Sheikh Hasina to leave the country. It thought that absence of these leaders from national scenes will encourage internal democracy within these parties. People of Bangladesh have welcomed the crackdown against the corrupt politicians. There was hardly any protest when several Bangladesh National Party Leaders and sons of Khaleda Zia, Tariq Rehman was arrested on charges of corruption and extortion.

If we look at the debates of Constituent Assembly we would be convinced that Indian leadership abhorred dynastic politics and never imbibed such a practice. Founding fathers of our constitution never conceived the idea that parliamentary system of government they were carving out will meet such an ugly fate with danger of corruption and nepotism looming large over the entire government set up. Those were the days when virtues like simplicity, integrity, candidness, lofty ideals and spirit of sacrifice were given weightage and not just dry caliber or family background. Leaders like Dr. Rajendra Prasad, Partabhi Sitaramayya, K.M. Munshi, G.V. Mavlankar, Sardar Vallabhbhai Patel, Maulana Azad, Rafi Ahmed Kidwai, Asaf Ali, Gulzari Lal Nanda, Pt. Govind Ballabh Pant and Dr. B.R. Ambedkar were leaders who were known for their high morals, sacrifice for freedom, virtues of self-less service and patriotism. Purity in personal and public life and accountability while holding government post were their other areas of concern. They remained absorbed in practising Indian ideals expressed in ancient literatures which proclaim:

> Na twaham kamaye rajyam, na sivargam na punarbhawam
> Kamaye dukh triptanam Praninamartnashnam.

(I neither desire to rule as king, nor heaven, nor re-incarnation. My only desire is to serve the people who are distressed, who are downtrodden.)

Sardar Patel was so much critical of family members' meddling in political matters that he dissuaded his son and daughter to even come to Delhi. When he had fallen ill after suffering from heart attack, his son Dahyabhai's son Bipin had come to visit him in Delhi to see his grandfather. Sardar didn't like son or grandsons visiting him while he was holding the post of Home Minister. He gave two pieces of advice to his grandson—One, "As long as I am in this chair don't visit Delhi." And second, "All sorts of people will contact you. Take care." Another example of stubborn resistance to family members reflects when Sardar Patel told his son Dahyabhai Patel not to come to meet him in connection with any personal work. The possibility that his son might seek or receive a favour in the capital incensed Sardar and he ordered Dahyabhai to return to Bombay. "Anger arose in me" Sardar told this to GD Birla a day or two later. Such was the astuteness and Spartan way of dealing with country, its people and the family. Leave aside promoting sons or daughters, they had imbibed the virtues of *Nishkam Karma* as propounded in Gita and virtually devoted their whole life to achieve highest perfection.

They could not imagine in their wildest dream that their three years' stupendous task of framing Constitution would be set at naught in 1975 just about 25 years after the Constitution coming into force, when it would be trampled upon to pave the way for smooth-sailing of dynastic perpetuation of Indian politics in the hands of Indira Gandhi, her son Sanjay Gandhi and caucus of few persons surrounding them. They could not imagine that this game of promoting families would go down deeper to pervert the constitutional institutions. Imagine a father, his son, his nephew together becoming members of Lok Sabha. (Refer Mulayam Singh Yadav, his son Akhilesh Yadav, his nephew Dharmendra Yadav all becoming members). Imagine further when a father-in-law joining Union Cabinet with his son-in-law as minister and son as Chief Minister of a State. (Reference Farooq Abdullah, son-in-law Sachin Pilot and son Omar Abdullah as Chief Minister). Wait for few years, it will be occupied by royals. Can it still be called as "Lok Sabha" even while dominated by such other family combinations? Time has changed the meaning and definition of words. If word "Lok" means "people" it is these royal "people" descended on earth through parachute and not "people coming out of soil". When 15th Lok Sabha has the largest number of father-son couples, nobody can deny that the coming Lok Sabhas and state legislative assemblies would be dominated by royal families finding the politics as more fecund and fertile as "family business". In his article "Family Matters" (*The Hindustan Times*) Vir Sanghvi wrote that India has become an oligarchy. Democracy is about choice and once you restrict the choice you destroy the very basis of democracy. In an another article "Politics of Inheritance" published in *The Hindustan Times*, he wrote that family-dominated politics is a closed shop. It is the birth and not the caliber which is the criteria. True democracy is replaced by a kind of feudalism in which the peasants are given the right to choose between various aristocrats. Another journalist Santosh Desai in his article "Dynasty: Undemocratic but alive and kicking" (*The Times of India*) wrote that Even the media glorifies the young leaders and champions their causes. Rahul Gandhi in particular is now being described in glowing terms without worrying too much about his dynastic roots. *The Times of India* in his editorial "Family Business" warned that the time has come for us to think about the centrality of family in Indian politics and call it our most significant contribution to political thought after Arthashastra. The phenomenon seems to suit the leadership and the cadre fine. The electorate has been generous in giving the stamp of approval if the number of MPs and MLAs from political families is any indication. The business of politics appears to be just another business with ownership passing from father to son as a matter of legacy. Family retainers also prefer it that way. And voters, do they have a choice except a Hobson's choice. Contesting election does not require just bags full of money but also a political clan or clout nurtured assiduously through a father or a godfather.

Working of dynastic politics in Philippines provide us an example how far democracy can be transformed into oligarchy. A look to its working is sure to erode our belief in proverb—democracy is a government of the people, for the people and by the people. There are no political parties but political families and about two-thirds of the lawmakers represent about 250 elite families. House of Representative is a meeting place of trapos where they work together primarily for their own interests and not really for the ideals of democracy. Instead of discussing the problems of the people they represent, the entire exercise remain over the interference in nominations, appointments and posting of favourable bureaucrats and lobbyism for political benefits. Dynastic politics is so deeply rooted in the political system that those who are born into a political dynasty can claim on inherent responsibility or preserved by family tradition to rule and those who are born under the rule of such a political dynasty seem to accept their destiny as such and consider political engagement as taboo. According to some historians, dynastic politics was introduced to the Philippines by the Americans not by the Spaniards. Electoral politics was initially limited to wealthy people and when the Americans left in 1946 wealthy landowners took the helm in leading the country to protect their business and other interest which was possible only by entering into politics. It hampered the possibility of developing in-built leadership coming from the people themselves. People themselves were divided in their approach and they accepted the declining system as *fait accomplie.* A yoke of tradition amongst people hampers any voice which can be raised against such an ugly political situation. It is a democracy of the families, for the families and by the families. Philippines acquired such a putrefied political system gradually over the years.

If we see the yoke of tradition on dynastic politics gaining momentum in India, it can be said with certainty that in the coming few decades, it will become absolutely difficult to even discuss political reform. Since leaders of every political party are under the grip of temptation to see their progeny well settled in politics, they are unlikely to oppose the system and this becomes the starting point of dynastic politics in this country.

To obviate the growing dynastic hegemony over Indian politics, no legal or constitutional provision can be made without controversy. Every individual has right to develop and establish in a profession of his choice and aptitude. No person can be debarred from entering into politics merely because his father or mother is occupying high political position. Nevertheless, it can also not be feasible if a family comprises a Council of Minister or a Chief Minister or a Prime Minister uses his influence and political position to groom political career of his son. Imagine a Cabinet headed by Father as Chief Minister while sons and daughters and other relatives as ministers. Will it be a Cabinet or a family limited firm? Our country's politics is surely on this track and it would not come as surprise in coming few decades if not years. Can any reasonable and right thinking person accept such abysmal burial of constitutional spirit. To save our polity from the present political malaise, the following provisions can be considered for incorporation in the Constitution and also some amendments in the Peoples Representation Act 1951:

1. No Council of Ministers either at the Centre or in the States shall have ministers who are related to each other by blood, marriage or adoption. Such provisions exist in countries like Brazil.
2. No Minister, Chief Minister or Prime Minister shall canvass for votes directly or indirectly in election where his son or any other relative by blood, marriage or adoption is contesting the election.
3. No person who is related to a Minister, Chief Minister or Prime Minister shall be allowed to contest from the constituency which falls within the constituency of that Minister, Chief Minister or Prime Minister. That is to say if 'X' is an MP from a constituency, his relative can not contest for assembly if the constituency of Legislative Assembly falls within the Parliamentary constituency of that MP.
4. If Minister, Chief Minister or Prime Minister has a son or daughter who is an MP from the same State, no discriminatory favour in release of fund for development works should be extended to his constituency as that would amount to granting favours. Election Commission or any other impartial

agency should be conferred with powers to supervise or see motives in such acts relating to grants for such constituencies.

5. No inauguration or foundation stone ceremony should be attended by CM, or PM in a constituency wherein his kin or relative is representative.
6. Code of Conduct for political parties must be re-framed with some clauses referring to above such measures.
7. The recommendation of National Commission for Review of the working of the Constitutional must be considered.
8. It is for Election Commission to consider such rules for code of conduct which can be implemented without necessitating legal or constitutional surgery. The above such measures can be taken by the Election Commission as it has powers under Constitution.

As leaders of almost every political party have their own axes to grind in the whole political scenario, it is unlikely that any discussion on the matter will yield fruitful outcome. All talks of reforms are bound to fall flat when nobody is willing to muster up to initiate talks for reforms. Now things are reaching to such a flashpoint where dynastic politics has started taking an ugly turn to derail the criminal justice system. It has brought even the government and administration under its spell of influence. As an example, a controversy over two-months parole to Manu Sharma son of Venod Sharma a former minister and a known politician of Haryana in October 2009 can be cited. Manu Sharma was convicted for murder of Jessica Lal and was serving life term. Ignoring as many as 80 similar applications pending for several months, Delhi Government, hastily granted him parole first for one month and then extended the period for another one month. It proved further that politicians can not see beyond the interests of their progeny and will not hesitate to arm-twist the rules, conventions and even the judicial system with gross impunity.

5

Women's Representation Bill—An Unresolved Controversy

Women, in spite of their comprising half of the population of the country are meagerly represented in Lok Sabha. They as voters constitute 340 million out of total 710 million voters in 2009 but constitutes a lowly 9 per cent of the total strength of 15th Lok Sabha. This unequal representation of women is disquieting. India ranks 134th among 183 countries in percentage of women legislators in Parliaments. According to data from the Inter-Parliamentary Union, India ranks 134th in terms of the percentage of women legislators in Parliament which is just 8.3 per cent of the total seats in 14th Lok Sabha. In terms of gender development too, India ranks 115th and is considered as patriarchal society. In comparison, the Parliament of Pakistan comprised 21.3 per cent women placing it at a highly respectable rank of 40. Although every Parliament all over the world has more males than females as members, Rwanda heads the list with an impressive 48.8 per cent of its Parliamentarians being women. Again, it is committed to sending at least 30 per cent women to its Parliament. Sweden has 45.3 per cent, Norway 38.2 per cent, Finland 37.5 per cent and Denmark 36.90 per cent. Even Iraq, an Islamic country, has 31.5 per cent women members followed by Syria 12 per cent, Indonesia 11.3 per cent, USA 15.2 per cent, Britain 19.7 per cent and France 12.2 per cent as women members.

Notwithstanding the Constitutional provisions eliminating the discrimination on the ground of sex and provisions under Directive Principles of State Policy for ameliorating the conditions of women, nothing substantial has been done to encourage women to contest and become members of Parliament. The 108th Constitution Amendment Bill which provides 33 per cent reservation on rotation basis through a lottery system began with the Prime Minister himself introducing it in Parliament. The Bill on its enactment and coming into force would result in two-thirds of the incumbent members forcibly unseated in every general elections and the remaining will be in limbo till the last moment. With a view to ensure adequate representation to women, the Select Committee recommended for rotation of seats over a period of three terms one-third seats for women can be ensured even in a State or Union Territory which has only one or two seats in the House of the People. The Bill remains badly mired into controversies and generated so much heat that once Sharad Yadav JD(U) MP, during debate in Lok Sabha stunned the House and the country by his unusual remark of eating poison if the Bill is passed in its present form. He remarked "We may not have the numbers but I will consume poison and die here but not allow the passage of the Women's Representation Bill." Another bitter criticism came from leader of Samajwadi Party Mr. Mulayam Singh who described the Bill as "dangerous" for the leadership of Lok Sabha. Terming it as a 'conspiracy', he said that the Bill in its present form would finish the leadership. Almost similar opinions were expressed by a large number of MPs who apprehend that the move, if comes into force, may fall upon the political careers taking the toll of nascent and vibrant leadership in the country.

In a historic move, nearly 15 years old Women Representation Bill to amend the Constitution was introduced in Rajya Sabha on 8th March, 2010 and passed on 9th March, 2010 amidst unprecedented vociferous protest followed by boycott of the sitting by members belonging to SP, BSP and RJD, etc. The Bill envisages amendment in Article 330 with an additional clause A(1) laying down the provision for reservation of women in the House of the People. It lays down further that not less than one-third of the total number of seats reserved under clause (2) of Article 330 shall be reserved for women belonging to the Scheduled Castes or, as the case may be, the Scheduled Tribes. Not less than one-third (including the number of seats reserved for women belonging to the Scheduled Castes and the Scheduled Tribes) of the total number of seats to be filled by direct election to the House of the People in a State or Union Territory shall be reserved for women and such seats may be allotted by rotation to different constituencies in that state or union territory. Article 332 A(1) lays down the provision for reservation of seats for women in the Legislative Assembly of every state. Such reservation for women shall, however, be reviewed after 15 years from the commencement of the Act giving an impression that the move is a transient measure only. But the past experience belies this assertion as we find reservation for SCs and STs which was originally provided for 10 years. The Bill shall require to be ratified by at least 50 per cent of the state assemblies before it can be brought on Statute Book.

The Women Reservation Bill is seriously flawed. The rotation of one-third seats will result in forcible unseating of two-thirds MPs every election. Remaining one-third members will be in limbo until last moment, not knowing whether or not their constituency will form part of the one-third randomly reserved seats and thus require them to scramble at short notice to find another seat to contest. Male members will find proxies in their wives and daughters and thus the move shall promote dynastic politics. The real objective of promoting women's cause will get diluted. A member, knowing that he is not sure to get re-elected shall neglect the constituency and thus a co-ordination between representative and people is bound to take a back seat. It will dampen the natural flow of leadership from grass roots level. The move of reservation of seats is against the principles of democratic representation as it will retard the nursing of constituencies by the prospective candidates. Another matter regarding the Constitutional validity of such an amendment which is violative of right to equality with equal protection of law and no discrimination on the ground of caste, creed and sex has not been debated at all. There are already a long catena of judgments wherein Supreme Court has held several laws, orders and notifications ultra vires to the Constitution on the ground of discrimination. There is no doubt that the bill shall be subjected to judicial scrutiny and its constitutional validity will enliven a national debate. It will open a vast field for lawyers to make a commentary.

The experience of fixed quotas in seats as prevalent in countries like Nepal, Philippines and erstwhile Soviet Union has not produced any successful results. In most of the Scandinavian countries such as Denmark, Norway and Sweden, the representation for women is even upto 42 per cent of the members. But it is due to the decisions of political parties themselves and not by legislative measures for mandatory reservation of seats. In Argentina there is a provision that a party must sponsor at least 42% candidates as women. If a party fails to do so, the list of candidates is not accepted by the electoral authorities. But the seats are not to be reserved. Similarly, in Belgium, where if a party fails comply with the gender composition, its list shall be refused by electoral authorities. No thought appears to have been given to such aspects while initiating women representation bill. The suggestion for making it mandatory for political parties to put up 33% of their candidates instead of reserving the seat has not been given any thoughtful consideration. China too has a higher representation for women in National Peoples Congress but without any quota policy. There are about 21 countries in which women representation is over 30 per cent but not by mandatory reservation of seats. Problem in our country is that there can never be a consensus on any issue. If the laws are made, these are made with flaws.

As the reservation is large, permanent reservation of certain seats is neither feasible nor politically permissible and that is why the Bill provides for rotation of reservation in every election. This rotation of reservation of seats will automatically result in two-thirds of incumbent members being forcibly unseated in every general elections (one-third reserved seats will become open seats and the same number will be reserved for women from open seats). The remaining one-third will be left in limbo until the last movement not knowing if their constituency will form part of the one-third randomly reserved seats. There is already resentment about reserved seats for SCs and STs being frozen in the same constituencies over a period of time. The population of SCs and STs is now estimated to be 16 per cent and 8 per cent respectively on all India basis. In the event of rotation of all reserved seats (women plus SCs plus STs) with one-third seats reserved for women, practically every single seat will be rotated in every general election. While male members knowing that their future hangs in balance on their constituencies being reserved for women, they may not take keen and energetic nursing of their constituencies. Similarly women members, knowing that on rotation their constituencies are unlikely to be reserved in coming election, they too would'nt nurture the constituencies and feel accountable in the manner in which they are doing at present. It is an axiom that it takes time for leadership to emerge through tedious paths. Hence flexibility promotes natural leadership. If the constituencies would be reserved and de-reserved on rotation basis, the flexibility and competitiveness are bound to adversely affected.

Answer therefore lies in ensuring that parties nominate a large number of women candidates. Therefore the amendment in Representation of Peoples Act 1951 can be considered to make it mandatory for every political party to put up women candidates for the required quota reserved for them. Such similar provisions can be considered for constituencies reserved for SCs and STs. Political parties can choose women candidates duly taking all factors whether local, national or social depending upon the ability and past performance of the candidate to whom they wish to present before the electorate.

The experience of fixed quotas for women in few countries where it has been tried such as Nepal, the Philippines and erstwhile Soviet Union has not produced very successful results for women's participation. It is noticed that wherever reservation of seats for women has been enforced, it is the proxies of their husbands or relatives who dominate the scene. It is felt that majority of seats reserved for women will be cornered by elite section of the society such as bureaucrats, politicians and big business houses. It will again be a mockery of a pious and august constitutional forum like Parliament making the remedy as worse than disease. Moreover, Bill is completely silence about women's representation in Rajya Sabha. It is ironical why other alternative measures like amendment in Peoples Representation Act 1951 for making it mandatory for political parties to put up one-third of their candidates as women in election could be considered. Parliament is a constitutional forum to debate national issues and reserving seats on gender basis and that too on rotation basis is bound to shatter the spirit enshrined in the Constitution.

6

Electoral Malpractices, Poor Polling and Illiteracy

Conducting elections in India is a gigantic task and involves massive mobilization of men, money and resources. The total budget for the Parliamentary elections in 2009 was set to a whopping Rs. 10,000 crores or $2 billion. Compare this with Barack Obama and other candidates spending which came close to $1.8 billion (nearly Rs. 8,000 crores) in the year long presidential election campaign in USA. The cost of general elections in India got doubled as compared to about Rs. 4,500 crores in election to 14th Lok Sabha in 2004. The figures do not include the amount of expenditure incurred by political parties and the candidates. No fair account can be presented on the amounts spent at all different levels. What we get in return is, hung house, instability and incidents of unholy alliances. In General Elections 2004, there stood 5,435 candidates for 543 seats. With 671.5 million voters and 6,87,402 polling stations, India's electoral system assumes a unique electoral battle nowhere to be experienced in any other country. The figures swelled to 714 million eligible voters registering a 6.4 per cent increase than 2004 general elections and 8,28,804 polling stations in 2009 General Elections. In 2009 general elections, 499 of total 543 constituencies were newly delimited with 20 per cent increase in polling booths. This entire expensive exercise is not without flaws and frictions. Elections are marked by violence, booth-capturing and poor polling, boycott of polling, controversies over candidates with criminal records and intimidation of voters etc.

In spite of number of measures introduced by Election Commission of India to check electoral malpractices, which the Election Commission receives, are over use of money power, bogus voting, misuse of official machinery including state-owned vehicles and helicopters, emotional appeals to voters in the name of caste or religion and inciting people on the basis of parochial or regional sentiments. Communal politics has reached its crescendo. The move of Andhra Pradesh Government to reserve five per cent of government jobs for Muslim community and Central Government move to enhance reservation of Muslim seats from 50 per cent to 75 per cent has added new dimension to the electoral politics. The move is likely to have a cascading effect as gradually other communities such as Christians, Parsis, Buddhists, Sikhs and Jains may also join the bandwagon top seek their share as they are also minorities and by no stretch of imagination they can be excluded from the reservations. Then polarization of votes on caste rather than rational consideration is another factor which leaves behind unhealthy trend in the political system of the country.

Poverty and illiteracy are other contributory factors which play their dominant role in weakening of the system. It is anticipated that there are 260 million people who live below poverty line. There are about 380 million children below the age of 14 for whom the arrangements for education is woefully inadequate. According to UNESCO'S World Monitoring Report 2005, India occupies top position with 33 crores illiterate people. Even China does not have such a low level of illiteracy and only 11 per cent of its population has been found illiterate. Neighboring countries like Pakistan and Bangladesh have only 6 per cent and 7 per cent population as illiterate.

The above factors together play their such dominant role that every political party tries hard to create vote bank by making appeal to their sentiments. Thus the caliber taking backseat, national interest suffer and parliament remains deprived of the highly talented and creamy intelligentsia which is manifest in the poor quality of debates. Politics is reduced to a scramble where it is either member of the family or caste or community which is to be represented.

Courts have from time to time laid stress on electoral reforms and passed several judgments giving guidelines for enforcing them. These have hit the headlines.

The then NDA Government at Centre brought out the 91st Constitution Amendment Bill seeking to contain the size of the Council of Ministers to 15 per cent of the Lower House in the case of the Centre and in the States. The Amendment Bill debar a defector from holding any "remunerative political post" for the remaining tenure of the legislature or unless re-elected. Passed by both the Houses of Parliament, the Bill received Presidential assent in January 2004 and the new law came on the Statute book in the name of the Constitution (Ninety-first Amendment) Act 2003. While this Constitution Amendment Act 2003 disallows defection by a legislature, it nevertheless permits bulk defection when one-third of the members of a party split from the parent group. The provisions to limit the size of the Cabinets and prevents defections were suggested long ago by Y.B. Chavan Committee in 1968 and Dinesh Goswami Committee in 1990. The recommendations made by Chavan Committee were considered harsh when it suggested that there must be an embargo on the induction of defectors in the cabinets or other offices of profit for six months.

Election Commission of India played its key role in Assemblies elections for five States in 2003. When the Notification for polls was issued on 7 November 2003, the Commission ensured the compliance of Model Code of Conduct in stricter and ruthless terms. Mr. J.M. Lyngdoh, the then Chief Election Commissioner warned the state governments against misuse of official machinery and also the government staff. He directed the Chief Secretary of Chhattisgarh Government to ensure that departmental officials were not posted in the constituencies where their minister was contesting. He even contemplated the deployment of government staff from other States for election duty in Chhattisgarh. Upset with the repeated complaints about violation of model code of conduct, Shri Lyngdoh openly declared that Jogi State is worse than Gujarat.

On receiving complaint that Chhattisgarh Chief Minister Ajit Jogi was using State aircraft for electioneering, the Election Commission sought details and found the contents of complaint true and confirmed. It issued a notice to the Congress to show cause why it should not be de-recognised for such a serious violation of model code of conduct. In reply, Congress admitted that the Chief Minister Ajit Jogi used the State aircraft twice between October 6 and October 12, 2003, the dates specified by the Election Commission in its Show Cause notice. But Congress took the plea that it was an "inadvertent error". Party said that the Chhattisgarh Chief Minister used the State aircraft only for official purposes because they had to reach 'far flung' areas. Even if there was a breach of model code of conduct, it was an inadvertent error and a *bona fide* mistake.

Within a week, Congress got another tough note from Election Commission. It censured the Congress for violating the model code of conduct by using state aircraft. It also issued another notice to the Congress to show cause why action to derecognize the national character of the Congress should not be initiated for the use of State-owned aircraft by Captain Amarinder Singh, Chief Minister of Punjab for electioneering from 15 November 2003 to 17 November 2003. This second notice plus censure came as a rude shock to the Congress party. Giving credence to the apprehensions raised by several political parties about large-scale bogus voting, Election Commission issued directives to Presiding Officers that they shall insist for Election Photo Identity Cards (EPIC) before permitting their holders to exercise franchise. In case they do not produce it before the Presiding Officer at the time of casting their ballot, they would'nt be permitted to vote. Though this move cause initial difficulties for the voters and the personnel conducting elections, it nevertheless came out to be a breather for those who were struggling hard to prevent such malpractices.

The Representation of People's Act 1951 lists out some corrupt practices which may on proved charges lead to the setting aside of the election. Section 123 of the Act lays down that corrupt practices would include bribery, any gift or promise by a candidate or his agent, undue influence, appeal to vote or refrain from voting for any person on the ground of his religion, race, caste, community or language to promote feeling of enmity or hatred, publication of any statement which is false, hiring or procuring of any vehicle by a candidate or his agent, incurring expenditure higher than the prescribed ceiling in contravention of Section 77 and booth capturing by a candidate or his agent or other person. However, such corrupt practices would be hit by this Section only when these are committed during the election campaign, i.e. after the date of filing of nomination. If the charge of indulging in corrupt practice is leveled pertaining to a period prior or preceding to the date of filing of nomination, the same can not be taken into consideration for judging the validity or legality of the election (*Subhash Desai* vs. *Sharad J. Rao AIR 1994 SC 2277*).

Declaration of assets and liabilities has been made a mandatory requirement for every elected candidate under the Representation of Peoples Act 1951. Section 75A lays down that such a declaration has to be made within ninety days from the date on which he makes and subscribes an oath or affirmation. Such a declaration shall be in respect of the movable and immovable property of which he, his spouse and his dependent children are jointly or severally owners or beneficiary, his liabilities to any public financial institution and his liabilities to the Central Government or the State Government. A candidate has to file account of election expenses. If he fails to lodge the account of election expenses within the time the Commission shall by order published in the official Gazette declare him to be disqualified for three years. In terms of latest guidelines issued by the Election Commission of India, a candidate at the time of filing nomination shall have to make a declaration that he does not have any amount or financial liability against Government on account of tax, charge, rent or any amount payable for use of electricity, telephone, repayment of loan and that he does not have any financial liability.

To check the corrupt persons from entering into legislatures through elections, Section 8 of the Representatives of Peoples Act 1951 provides that a person convicted of any offence and sentenced for not less than two years shall be disqualified from the date of such conviction and shall continue to be disqualified for a further period of six years since his release. Section 9 provides that a person who having held an office under the Government of India or under the Government of any State has been dismissed for corruption or for disloyalty to the State shall be disqualified for five years from the date of such dismissal. Similarly, a person shall be disqualified if there subsists a contract entered into by him in the course of his trade or business with the appropriate Government for the supply of goods to, or for execution of any works undertaken by the Government.

The nexus between black money and elections is not of recent origin. It was referred to by the Direct Taxes Enquiry Committee (Wanchoo Committee) Report 1971. It made several recommendations to curb the use of black money in elections. However, the recommendations, though practical and workable besides being acceptable to all the political parties, were deferred for the reasons that these were potential enough to be counter-productive to the electoral fortunes of the Congress party. Shri M.C. Chagla went to the extent of saying that Legislators, in fact, represent money power rather than the people. The N.I.P.F.P. (The National Institute of Public Finance and Policy) in its report *Black Money in India* had shown how black money had come to acquire a powerful niche in Indian political system.

In an another move to prevent use of black money in 2004 General Elections, Election Commission took an unusual step by directing the Ministry of Civil Aviation to step up vigil at all airports to keep tabs on cash being transported as part of passenger baggage. This led to the recovery of Rs. 51 lacs cash at Bhubaneshwar Airport from an employee of a corporate house. This recovery rattled all political parties and realization dawned upon them that excessive and unabashed use of black money may prove to be counter productive upsetting their whole game plan. With a view to check money power from influencing electors, the Election Commission came out with ceilings on election expenses. It issued an order under Conduct of Election Rules 1961 on 24th October 2003 vide which maximum ceiling for election expenses for parliamentary and assembly constituencies was fixed State-wise as under:

Table 6.1: Maximum Election Expenses Under Conduct of Election Rules 1961

Sl. No.	Name of State	Maximum limit of election expenses in any one	
		Parliamentary Constituency	Assembly Constituency
1.	Andhra Pradesh	25,00,000	10,00,000
2.	Arunachal Pradesh	17,00,000	6,00,000
3.	Assam	25,00,000	10,00,000
4.	Bihar	25,00,000	10,00,000
5.	Goa	14,00,000	5,00,000
6.	Gujarat	25,00,000	10,00,000
7.	Haryana	25,00,000	10,00,000
8.	Himachal Pradesh	25,00,000	7,00,000
9.	Jammu & Kashmir	25,00,000	—
10.	Karnataka	25,00,000	10,00,000
11.	Kerala	25,00,000	10,00,000
12.	Madhya Pradesh	25,00,000	10,00,000
13.	Maharashtra	25,00,000	10,00,000
14.	Manipur	22,00,000	5,00,000
15.	Meghalaya	22,00,000	5,00,000
16.	Mizoram	20,00,000	5,00,000
17.	Nagaland	25,00,000	5,00,000
18.	Orissa	25,00,000	10,00,000
19.	Punjab	25,00,000	10,00,000
20.	Rajasthan	25,00,000	10,00,000
21.	Sikkim	17,00,000	5,00,000
22.	Tamil Nadu	25,00,000	10,00,000
23.	Tripura	25,00,000	5,00,000
24.	Uttar Pradesh	25,00,000	10,00,000
25.	West Bengal	25,00,000	10,00,000

26.	Chhattisgarh	25,00,000	10,00,000
27.	Uttaranchal	25,00,000	7,00,000
28.	Jharkhand	25,00,000	10,00,000
	Union Torritories		
1.	Andaman & Nicobar Islands	17,00,000	—
2.	Chandigarh	14,00,000	—
3.	Dadra and Nagar Haveli	10,00,000	—
4.	Daman and Diu	10,00,000	—
5.	Delhi	25,00,000	8,00,000
6.	Lakshadweep	10,00,000	—
7.	Pondicherry	20,00,000	5,00,000

Every candidate has to keep a separate account of entire expenditure in connection with election campaigns. Such an account must be correct showing expenditure incurred by his election agent also. However, certain expenditures incurred by leaders of a political party on account of their travel by air or by any other means of transport for propagating programme of the political party shall not be deemed to be the expenditure in connection with the election incurred or authorized by a candidate of that political party or his election agent. Similarly, any expenditure in respect of any arrangement made, facilities provided or any other act done by any person in the service of the Government in the discharge or of his official duty shall not be deemed to be expenditure in connection with the election incurred. According to explanation added to Section 77 of the Representation of Peoples Act 1951, the leaders of a political party here mean the leaders of a recognized political party. In case of a political party which is not a recognized party, then such an exclusion of expenditure would be available for persons not exceeding twenty in number. According to Section 78, every contesting candidate at an election shall, within thirty days from the date of election of the returned candidate shall lodge with the District Election Officer an account of the election expenses which shall be a true copy of the account kept by him or by his election agent under Section 77.

Since not filing of account of election expenses or incurring an expenditure over and above the prescribed limit amounts to corrupt practices, it is laid down under Section 10A that the Election Commission can disqualify any person for a period of three years if he fails to lodge an account of election expenses within the time and in the manner required by or under the Act. Election Commission has the powers under Section 11 to remove the disqualifications or reduce the period of any such disqualifications. In the case of *G.R. Gulve* vs. *S.P. Aner AIR 1999 SC 3358,* a returned candidate charged to have distributed money to electors in a meeting to solicit votes. It was alleged that son of returned candidate had attended the meeting. The allegation was denied. Petitioner could not lead enough evidence to connect the returned candidate with allegations. Supreme Court held that such a vague and cryptic evidence can not form the basis for disqualifying an elected representative. Similarly, in another case of *C. Narayanaswamy* vs. *C.K. Jaffar Sharief 1994 AIR SCW 3799*, the petitioner alleged that elected candidate had organized mass feeding for electors to influence them and win electoral favour for him. However, the charge was countered on the ground that such mass feeding was arranged by the candidate against background of assassination of top leader of his party. Court held that mass feeding during the course of election can not be a ground to disqualify an elected representative if such programmes were conducted in pursuance to death of a leader of the political party. Such an expenditure would not, therefore, count towards the election expenses. It is important to mention that an act to fall within the meaning of corrupt practice must be related to pre-voting stage and not post-voting stage. In the case of *Dharamvir* vs. *Amar Singh AIR 1996 SC 2314,* it was held that Section 123(2) and Section 123(7) of the Representation of Peoples Act 1951 deal with corrupt practices indulged at a stage prior to the casting of votes. If an act is done to please the voters with whatever extravagance to celebrate victory, etc. after the elections are over, the same shall not count towards corrupt practice. A question arose as to whether news item published in the newspapers or any material published by the Advertising agency can be an evidence admissible for purpose of proving corrupt practice. In the case of *Qamarul Islam* vs. *S.K. Kanta AIR 1994 SC 1733* it was held that newspaper reports by themselves are not evidence to support the charge of corrupt practice. Newspaper reports are at the best secondary evidence without proper proof under the Evidence Act. Where the speech alleged to be delivered by the returned candidate during election campaign was published in a newspaper but neither the report who heard the speech and sent the report was examined nor even his reports produced, the production of the newspaper by the Editor and Publisher by itself can not amount to the contents of the newspaper reports.

During the course of intensive election campaigns, corrupt practices may be indulged in by persons who are neither the election agent of the candidate nor have his prior consent. It has been held by Supreme Court in the case of *Samant N. Balakrishna* vs. *George Fernandes AIR 1969 SC 1201* that direct or circumstantial evidence is necessary to prove that the elected candidate had consented to the act. Mere knowledge or connivance or similarities of ideas not enough to infer consent. To establish corrupt practice, by an agent other than election agent, avoiding the election, the consent on the part of returned candidate to the commission of corrupt practice must be proved. Though it is difficult to prove the consent directly given by the candidate. But the circumstances must point unerringly to the conclusion and must not admit of any other explanation.

Hiring or procuring of vehicles for free conveyance of voters has been held as corrupt practice under Section 323(5). In order to constitute such hiring of vehicles as corrupt practice, it is essential to prove that the vehicle hired was for ferrying the voters to the polling booths and secondly it was free of charge. If these ingredients are proved, then the charge of resorting to corrupt practice can be successfully alleged. In the case of *Dhartipakar* vs. *Rajiv Gandhi AIR 1987 SC 1577,* Supreme Court held that where the allegations did not contain any pleading regarding hiring of the vehicles by the elected candidate or any of his worker with his consent for conveyance of the voters to and from polling stations free of cost the charge did not make out a case of corrupt practice.

In cases where excessive expenditure in excess of limit is alleged or it is found that candidate has suppressed the fact of use of vehicle and failed to produce the account of expenditure, an inference can be drawn that he had committed corrupt practice. In the case of *R.P. Alithithan* vs. *P.H. Pandian AIR 1996 SC 1599: 1996*, Supreme Court held that an adverse inference can be drawn from the omission to produce the account that the candidate had committed corrupt practice. Such a conclusion on the basis of evidence on record, can not be said to be vitiated by any error of law. Likewise, in the case of *G.K. Bapat* vs. *Dattaji Raghobaji Meghe AIR 1995 SC 2384*, Supreme Court held that expenditure incurred by third person not authorized by candidate can not be held to be a corrupt practice. Therefore, in order to be a corrupt practice, the excessive expenditure must be incurred or authorized by the candidate or his election agent. An expenditure incurred by a third person which is not authorized by the candidate or his election agent is not a corrupt practice.

Voters' apathy and indifference towards elections is one of the various infirmities of electoral system. Obviously this is not a healthy situation for a country which claims to be the largest democracy in the world. When people are provided with a Constitutional right and they do not avail of it, it presents an anomalous situation. You can take the horse to water but can not make him to drink. There is hardly any democracy in the world wherein such an enormous 40 per cent people remain indoors on the date of elections. This apart from the fact that electoral rolls are always to be full of errors, deletion of names of eligible citizens while enrolment of dead or people who have already left to settle down elsewhere. During 1998 General Elections, Election Commission of India took a daring decision to exclude about 3.70 lakh voters from the electoral rolls in Assam on the ground of disputed citizenship. Supreme Court refused to stay the decision of the Commission. According to a survey conducted by Lok Satta, the overall error margin in electoral rolls exists from 18 to 20 per cent. This is in addition to 21% votes which are estimated to be polled as bogus. With such a huge error margin, the fate of a candidate can not remain without affected. Since margin of victory in election is often low, such a huge error margin in electoral rolls is found to tilt favour or disfavour among any of the candidates. With such a huge 18-20% errors in electoral rolls compounded further by about 21 per cent bogus voting, the existing electoral system can not be termed as fair or fool-proof and an election of a candidate may be mere technical. About one crore staffs including armed forces, para-military forces and civilian staff on poll duty are deprived of the right to vote due to pressure of work and other practical reasons. Under such a system, full representation of people can not be deemed to be taking place. A large number of countries in the world have adopted the method of proportional representation to eliminate the disproportionate number of seats against percentage of votes polled. The Election Commission should consider the website facility to display the Electoral rolls so that voters can themselves check their names and if any error is found, can file objections within a framework of time. This website facility to display the electoral rolls will make the task of scrutiny by the political parties easier. The error margin can be reduced substantially if not eliminated altogether. To prevent bogus voting, deterrent punishment should be provided and furnishing of proof of residence can be made essential.

In several democracies, such as Australia, Belgium, Brazil, Argentina, Bolivia, Chile, Costa Rica, Cyprus, Ecuador, EL Salvador, Finland, Greece, Mexico and Turkey, etc. provisions have been made for compulsory voting. A person abstaining from exercise of franchise would be deprived of some of the privileges that a citizen possesses. Pecuniary punishments have been provided which are to be recovered from voters who do not turn up to cast their vote. In Brazil, voting is compulsory for persons over eighteen years of age. It is optional only in case of illiterate persons and persons' over seventy years of age. Similarly, Constitution of Belgium provides that ballot is 'obligator' and 'secret'.

In a country like India, compulsory voting can be considered by providing incentives package. Fine for not voting may not be implementable for it requires tremendous exercise and people find various ways to escape from pecuniary fines. Some incentives which can be introduced to increase voting percentage may include:

1. Issuance of a Certificate/slip indicating name and serial number on voter list to the voter. Such a certificate may be asked for as an essential document while renewing Food Card, Driving Licence or for the purpose of taking admission into Government Hospital or admitting children in Government schools.
2. A person having certificate of voting should be preferred for grant of welfare schemes announced by Social Welfare Department of the Governments.
3. Such certificate must be made essential for getting Passport issued or renewed. Rules can be framed in this regard.
4. Government and Public Undertaking under its control often take up welfare program and registration schemes for housing and auctioning of plots, etc. A provision can be made wherein an applicant shall have to furnish a copy of certificate of voting. By doing this, it will send a message to all the voters that it is also in their own interests to exercise right to vote.
5. Similarly, while issuing PAN, Income Tax authorities can ask the assessee to furnish such a certificate as an additional evidence.

However, the condition of furnishing certificate of voting may be imposed on such persons only who acquired voting rights on the date of last election or five years whichever is earlier.

The above proposal, however, met with resistance on the ground that the freedom of expression implies both the rights, i.e. the right to express an opinion and also the right not to express opinion. If an individual chooses not to vote it is an assertion of his right not to express an opinion because voting is a way of expressing an opinion in regard to worthiness of the candidate. But the argument is wholly fallacious and does not carry conviction because in India, voters often do not exercise their right to vote out of their indifferent attitude rather than a conscious and deliberate attitude. Moreover, casting vote in an election falls within the ambit of fundamental duty and is not subjected to the right of not expressing opinion. If the people do not vote, they do not because of their lack of political awareness, lack of interest towards issues confronting the nation as a whole and not because of any considered opinion or conscious decision to refrain from voting. Sometimes, the longer distance from the residence to the polling station or long queue of voters prevail as specious grounds to remain indoor. So this can not be taken as a case of conscious decision not to vote. If the Government incurs huge expenditure on conducting elections, it is not worthwhile for the people to remain indifferent to a solemn duty towards nation and its polity.

Conducting and monitoring of General Elections in India is as gigantic a task as holding of polls in Europe, the United States, Canada and Australia all put together. Managing about nine lakh polling booths with the assistance of about one crore staffs including police personnel and para-military forces and preparation of election materials to enable nearly 710 million voters constitute an amazing feat which the whole world watches with utmost curiosity. Such a massive exercise can not be undertaken on the same day as we usually witness in other countries. Elections are conducted in phased manner to enable forces to move from State to State and ensure fair and peaceful elections. It has been a grievance from the employees and armed forces that under such tremendous pressure poll related duties and mobilization, they are deprived of the right to cast their vote. Various methods like postal ballots have not been found effective and a staff assigned with poll duties finds it enormously difficult to procure postal ballots which are often not made available easily. The practice of allowing the staff to use postal ballot has not been found encouraging due to practical difficulties in identifying the name on the voter list where a staff resides, then to requisition the postal ballot and then to send it confidentially to the concerned Returning officer. This whole exercise is too cumbersome to opt for. Only alternative that has been found more simple is to allow Proxy Vote and a staff on poll duty may be sending a prescribed form under his signature can name the person of his choice to exercise his right to vote on his behalf. The proposal is to permit the service voter to authorize any adult member of his right to vote on his behalf. The proposal is to permit the service voter to authorize any adult member of his family to vote for on his behalf in his native place. Although the proposal found workable, the same has not been introduced for implementation.

In 1963, the then Chief Election Commissioner had himself recommended to the Government for introducing compulsory voting on the pattern of electoral system currently in vogue in Brazil, Australia, Belgium and Argentina, etc. A voter who does not exercise his franchise without plausible reason like sickness, etc. is penalized. Such measures result in 90 per cent polling. Another measure which can be considered is e-voting which is adopted by Finland and Estonia. There are about six crores internet users in the country and if e-voting is permitted through UID (Unique Identity Card) it will result in increase in voting and substantial saving of expenditure paving a way for a truly largest democracy. However, lack of will and policy of ad-hocism has not let the electoral reforms be implemented fully.

While introducing Parliamentary system of Government, the framers of the Constitution adopted the Westminster based *First Past The Post* (FPTP System). The fact that this system is successful only in those democracies where two-party system exists. In U.K. this system poses no difficulty because there are two political parties. Whereas in our country, the existence of multi party system has wreaked havoc on the whole electoral exercise because under the present system a candidate getting minority votes is declared elected. In large number of States around 85% to 90% of the legislators have won on minority vote (i.e. by having obtained less than 50% of the votes cast. A large number of winning candidates were declared elected even though the voters polled by them was less than 20% of the votes cast. In Uttar Pradesh, over the last three assembly elections an average of only 90% legislators won on a minority votes. The same proposition for Bihar is 82%, for Madhya Pradesh 60%, for Assam 71% and for Karnataka 69% of the candidates won by securing minority votes. While introducing the parliamentary system from U.K., we forgot that it works mainly in communion with a two-party system or where there are limited number of politics. The pros and cons of FPTP system in the context of India's political system were not weighed to an optimum level. The Law Commission took this issue seriously and proposed "List System" in addition to the FPTP system. With a view to generate better representation by providing seats to recognized political parties in proportion to the votes obtained by them, it suggested for an increase in number of MPs in Lok Sabha by 25% and this additional number of MPs should be made up of candidates pre-nominated by political parties and the number should be in accordance with their share of the votes polled. This way the number of seats in Lok Sabha would be increased to 688 with about 138 candidates nominated on the basis of a list to be provided by various political parties. However, far from implementing the suggestion, it was not even debated upon for arriving at any logical decision. The doubts were, however, expressed that introduction of 'list system' simultaneously with the FPTP system would create two classes of members of Parliament in Lok Sabha—those elected directly by the people and those coming through party lists. But the fact that it would remove the anomaly caused by FPTP system is ignored by criticizing the suggestion made by Law Commission.

It would have been a better proposition if the suggestion made by Law Commission, to introduce list system without doing away with FPTP system, is introduced in any State on trial basis to find out the actual representation on the ground level. However, there is no final proposal from the Government or the Election Commission of India to this effect.

The National Commission to Review the Working of The Constitution, in its Report submitted on 31st March 2002 has made the following suggestions:

1. Debar all legislators from being appointed as chairpersons of various state undertakings, also debar them from any non-ministerial post other than chairmanship of legislative committees.
2. There must be a bar on ministries that are larger than 10 per cent of the house. No other position with executive or financial powers to be considered for legislators. Also, the power to create minister level or cabinet rank post should be strictly regulated.
3. There must be a limit of two-terms for any political position. So one may be a member of the Panchayat for two terms, of State Assembly only for two terms even if non-contiguous and M.P. for two terms. This may reduce the number of life-time professional politicians who have no other sources of livelihood except political office.
4. The Election Commissioner should be appointed by a neutral body consisting of the Prime Minister, the Vice President, the Speaker, the leader of the Opposition and the Chief Justice of India. This would make his position totally impartial in the eyes of political parties factions. The Election Commissioner should not be appointed to any other office after retirement.
5. An independent auditing authority should be appointed for auditing annual statement of accounts of all political parties and the audited accounts should be published for public scrutiny.
6. Rotation of seats should be done for SC seats and non-schedule area ST seats.
7. There seems to be a general agreement on the need to have women members. The question is whether the political parties should be asked to put up women candidate for at least one-third of the seats they contests both for the State and Parliament elections or one-third seats should be reserved for them by rotation. Another suggestion made is that there may

be a 30 per cent increase in the number of seats in the house and these additional seats be filled by women candidates on the basis of a "List System".

8. The minimum number of valid votes polled should be increased to 25 per cent in order to forfeit the deposit. Also, the amount of deposit should be again increased substantially. These two steps would further reduce non-serious candidates.
9. All candidates should be required to clear all government dues, e.g. huge I.T. arrears before their candidature is accepted. This pertains also to the holding on the accommodation of the telephones and government facilities while in power.
10. Election Commissioner should have full disciplinary authority over the officials who are involved in election duties. It is said that at present there are too many complaints of compromised or partisan officials but Election Commission is unable to take any stringent action. The question however is whether the Election Commission could have the same disciplinary powers over all the officers and staff engaged on election duty as that of the appointing authority.
11. Create multi-member or double-member constituencies to eliminate or at least reduce narrow appeals based on religion or caste.
12. Hold State level and parliamentary level elections at the same time. This would reduce expenditure.
13. Every candidate to an elected office at the time of filing of nomination and every holder of a political position annually must declare his assets and liabilities as also the assets and liabilities of his close family members.
14. For legislative councils, eliminate the teachers' and graduates' constituencies, which provide extra votes to some electors and have politicized educational institutions.

15. Subsequent to the 73rd and 74th Amendments, ensure that criminalization does not engulf our Representative Institutions and there must be serious debate on the issue with a view to substantive reforms.
16. For contesting elections to the Rajya Sabha the requirement of the candidate being 'ordinarily resident' in the state should be interpreted to mean that he or she should be actually residing in that state.

Other reform options to tackle different problems broadly within the existing electoral system are summed up below:

Electoral rolls and identity cards

1. Electoral Rolls should be updated at the lowest constituency level with a clear link to the higher constituency levels till the parliamentary constituency.
2. There should be a mechanism for constantly updating these rolls and during each first week of April the updated rolls as of 31st December of the previous year should be posted on the web.
3. Multi-purpose voters identity cards or citizenship cards should be designed with a bar coded unique voter identity number. Over an acceptable period of time these should become mandatory for all elections.
4. This job should be entrusted to a pre-qualified professional organizations and should include designing, the implementation of the scheme of the scheme in coordination with and under the Election Commission. Representatives Institutions and local post offices to be involved in helping in its implementation.
5. The designing of electoral rolls and ID should be co-ordinated with a view to the future.
6. The responsibility for the electoral rolls and ID should rest with one integrated machinery under the EC/SECs.

Electronic voting machines

7. Introduce Electronic Voting Machines in all constituencies as rapidly as possible for all sensitive constituencies use them straightway.

Booth-capturing and rigging

8. Reference Section 58A of the Representation of Peoples Act 1951, give Election Commission the authority to take decision regarding booth capturing not only on the report of the Returning Officer but even otherwise if it is satisfied.
9. Under Section 58A of the Act, the Election Commission should not only be empowered to countermand the Election and order a fresh election as now provided under the law, but also should be empowered to declare the earlier poll to be void and order only a re-poll in the entire constituency, instead of a re-election there, depending on the nature and seriousness of each case.
10. Make booth-capturing punishable with more stringent punishment and empower the election commission, to investigate booth-capturing and other violations of the electoral law, through the Central or State police investigating agency; by the establishment of special electoral courts.
11. Consider use of tamper-proof video and other electronic surveillance at sensitive polling stations/ constituencies.

Caste and communal hatred

12. Any campaign on the basis of caste or religion and any attempt to spread caste and communal hatred during elections should be punished with immediate disqualification and mandatory imprisonment.

President's rule during elections

13. Chief Election Commissioner's suggestion to impose President's Rule over all the States for the duration of the elections may not be considered logical or feasible.

Criminalisation

14. Once charges relating to certain crimes have been framed by a court against a person, he should not be permitted to contest elections unless cleared.
15. A potential candidate against whom charges have been framed by the police may take the matter to a special electoral court. This court would be obliged to enquire and take a decision in a strictly time bound manner. Basically, this court may decide whether there is indeed a prima facie case justifying the framing of charges. If yes, the person should not be allowed to contest.
16. Eliminate incongruities in the existing provisions of Sub-section (1), (2) and (3) of Section 8 of the Representation of the People Act 1951, whereby a rapist convicted and sentenced to 10 years imprisonment, may be disqualified only for six years under Sub-section (1) and thus remains free to contest elections, even while in prison serving the last four years of his sentence. The law should provide that whoever is convicted of any offence by a court of law and sentenced to imprisonment for six months or more should be debarred from contesting elections, for a period totaling the sentence imposed plus an additional six years.
17. Under Section 8(4), sitting members are not disqualified even when convicted until their appeal is decided. This should be deleted.
18. If an elected representative gets convicted on charges related to specific crime he should be required to withdraw from the legislature for six months and within that period he fails to get an acquittal he should be disqualified.
19. Political parties, when they are seen to be abetting criminalization should face de-recognition and other action.

Disqualification on ground of corrupt practices-election petition

20. Amend corrupt practice that once the High Court hands out the judgment on an election petition holding the candidate guilty of corrupt practice, the case goes to the Secretary of the concerned State Legislature or the Secretary General of Lok Sabha or Rajya Sabha, as the case may be. It is then forwarded to the President who in turn forwards to the Election Commission. Only then does the Election Commission gets the jurisdiction to tender its opinion to the President based on which the disqualification order is issued. Instead of this round about procedure, a direct reference between the High Court, the Election Commission and the President should be created to cut unnecessary delay.

21. Creates special electoral court for deciding on election petition. These should be decided in a time bound way within 6 to 12 weeks unlike the present where it can take years by which time they have lost their meaning.

Election expenditure—High cost of elections and views of unaccounted money power

22. The basic problem is that the present rule have a significant loophole in the shape of explanation I to Section 77(1) of the Representation of Peoples Act 1951, under which the amounts spent by the persons other than the candidate and his agent themselves, are not counted in his election expenses. This means there can never be any violation of expenditure limits. All extra expenditure, even when known and proven, can be shown to have been spent by the party or by any friend and it remains outside of the enforceable limits. This must be rectified and all expenditure made by or on behalf of the candidate must be included in his expenditure limit as provided under the rules.

23. Political parties as well as individual candidates should be subject to a proper statutory audit of the amounts they spend. At the end of the elections, each candidate should submit an audited statement of expenses, headwise. The audit should not only be mandatory but it should be enforced by the Election Commission appointing a counsel of at least two auditors say for 10 constituencies each. Any violation or misreporting should be dealt with strongly.
24. Partial State Funding of Elections through time provided on national media for campaign activities of recognized parties may continue.
25. For other proposed state funding, it has to be linked to the political parties being regulated by law and to creating a fool-proof mechanism to implement financial limits strictly and to deter expenditure violations.
26. Bring in transparency into all political funding.
27. Permit Corporate donations within prescribed limits and keep them transparent.
28. Make all legal and transparent donations, tax, exempt and treat this tax loss to the state as its contribution to State funding of elections. For example, tax exemption could be limited to say 2,50,000 to individual and 10 lakhs for companies provided that the contributions are made to party funds and not to individual. In the case of corporate contribution, the Board of Directors may approve upto say one lac and anything over this amount may be approved by the shareholders. Political funding should be separate head in the accounts and annual reports of the companies. This will ensure transparency.
29. All political parties' accounts, much like the accounts of the public companies should be published yearly with complete disclosure under predetermined accounts heads. The Election Commission should have these accounts audited.

30. Also make it obligatory for campaign expense accounts—both receipt and expenses—of all candidates to be made public in their constituencies.
31. There should be a serious attempt at reducing election expenses and this can be done by perhaps changing the ground rules for Electoral Campaigns—partly by encouraging the use of electronic and digital technology at state cost and simultaneously by totally and effectively banning other overt and wasteful tamashas of campaigning.

Run Off Method

Apart from above measures to reform the electoral system, the Commission has recommended Run-Off election method to ensure election of a candidate by a majority vote. Under this system, a re-poll is ordered in the event of no candidate getting more than 50 per cent votes and except the two candidates getting maximum votes, names of all the remaining candidates are deleted and in second round of election the contest remains between the two candidates only. In my opinion this system would make the matter worse for the reason that second round of poll may not attract the same number of voters who exercised their voting rights on the main election date. This may even imbalance the result and a winner may be loser. Further, organizing second round of election by fixing a date and telling voters to exercise their franchise again would be painstaking, exhaustive and may lead to the mockery of the whole election process and hence this part of recommendation, though ideally appreciable, may not receive a practical touch in successful terms.

The Commission's other recommendations include delimitation of constituencies to remove the anomalies and difference in number of voters Constituency-wise. The anomalies were removed when exercise of delimitation of constituencies was completed before elections to 15th Lok Sabha. However, widespread apprehensions were raised over the enormous increase in electorates to be represented by a legislation. It is obviously an uphill task for an MP to effectively represent the aspiration of a huge electorate without enhancing the number of seats in Lok Sabha. Hence demands are being raised to increase the number of seats so that MPs are not overburdened and people also find it convenient to contact their representatives for getting their demands pursued vigorously. But what is most important aspect in the whole arena is the steep reduction in number of Parliament's sittings. Unless the number of sittings are increased substantially and some disincentive measures are introduce to curb absenteeism in the proceedings of House, not much can be expected by just increasing the number of seats.

7

Multiplicity of Political Parties

Party system in a democracy is a projection of socio-economic and political factors. Its role in political affairs of a country holds special significance because it is the system which infuses life into the whole set up and galvanise the public opinion to activate the political framework. The whole political system is inconceivable without them. However, like any other system, it is not free from maladies and infirmities. A study of six decades long Parliamentary democracy in India would reveal that factors like plurality, diversity, uneven economic growth, regional sentiments and even caste or religious affiliations have together played dominant role to make room for multiparty system. It would also reveal that for about four decades, country remained under *One Party Rule* mainly because votes against it were divided among candidates of different parties in elections.

It is characteristic of Parliamentary system that small political parties finding their roots on regional consideration come to dictate their terms for joining a coalition government or supporting it from outside. A party winning just one or two seats acquires a clout in formation of a coalition government with all the possibilities to take ministerial berths. Today it is the political expediency rather than ideology that has come to stay as a dominating factor in a party system. The conglomeration of political parties in the name of *Fronts* like *United Front, Third Front or United Progressive Alliance* provide another unique feature of our party system. A Front is formed by parties with a view to prevent either the Congress or

BJP from coming into power. So Front has more negative than a positive goal. While *National Democratic Alliance* is formed to prevent Congress, *United Progressive Alliance* is formed to prevent BJP from coming into power. In countries where Presidential form of government is prevailing, multi-party system is not to be found. It is so because narrow, regional or parochial basis can not lead to emergence of a national plank when the entire electorate of the country is to elect one person as President. There are no front no alliance.

As per details made available by Election Commission, there are six National Political Parties, 45 State Political Parties and 702 un-recognised registered parties. Together there are 753 political parties in India out of which only 150 or so put up candidates for General Elections in 1998. With 671.5 million voters and such a long list of political parties we call India a largest democracy. The ever-increasing growth of Political Parties is also because there are no conditions under Representation of Peoples Act 1951 to deny registration to a political party. Section 29A of the Act states no such condition and Election Commission can not deny registration to a political party if it subscribes to the ideological perceptions referred to under Section 5. Another flaw or infirmity in the system is that once registered, a political party would stay registered in perpetuity even if it does not contest election. There is no specific provision to de-register a political party. Section 29A provides that any association or body of individual citizen of India calling itself a political party can make an application to the Election Commission for registration as a political party. However, according to the proviso to Section 29A of the Act, no association or body shall be registered as a political party unless the memorandum or rules and regulations of such association or body express true faith and allegiance to the Constitution of India as by law established and to the principles of socialism, secularism, unity and integrity of India. The Act does not prescribe minimum number of membership nor provides conditions to deny registration. Registration of political parties was brought under legal necessity when Parliament passed amendment introducing new section through an Amendment Act which came into force on 15th June 1989. Prior to June 1989, political parties were being registered under paragraph 3 of the Election Symbols (Reservation and Allotment) Order 1968. Commission has the power under Sub-section 6 of Section 29A to call for such other particulars as it may deem fit from the association or body.

A characteristic which is peculiarity of political parties in India is that these have splitted into different splintered groups to subsequently acquire the different names. Some political parties have merged too. Congress Party, Janata Party, Lok Dal, Communist Party, Dravadia Munnetra Kazhagam, Akali Dal, and Janata Dal have all faced divisions repeatedly on number of occasions. Congress party has faced the maximum number of splits. Today there are several Congresses such as Nationalist Congress Party, Trinamool Congress, Himachal Vikas Congress and Indian National Congress. The Communist party had undergone three splits. Today left parties are divided as CPI, CPI(M) and Forward Bloc. If they are combined to forge an alliance, it is not because of any burial of their policies but because of their one point programme of preventing right-wing parties led by BJP to stage a comeback to power. The fact which holds special significance in this regard is that these splits or divisions have not been on the basis of ideological differences but on the basis of clashes of interest and rather clashes of personality. Every political party has to build up personality cult to survive. Congress party which depends solely upon Nehruvian dynasty for its survival, has always needed a leader to rouse rhetorical and hysterical appeal among the masses. It leaves no scope for any other leader except drawn from Nehru dynasty to acquire a top slot position.

In the first General Elections held in 1952, nearly 192 Political parties sought recognition from the Election Commission. However it could recognize 14 All India and 52 State parties for the allocation of symbols. In the 1957 General Election, a criteria was adopted under which a political party was to secure at least three per cent votes polled in the preceding election. On the basis of this criteria only four national parties and 12 State parties could be recognized. In the third General Elections 1962, the Commission recognized nine All India parties and seven State parties on the basis of same criteria. The way political parties behaved in the post independence era and indulged in all sorts of fair or foul activities to either gain power or remain in power has demolished the faith of the people in the system. For them democracy is the game of 49 versus 51 and there is no equation which the money can not change. No political party ever maintained a fair account of its income and expenditure. The donations from companies were seldom reflected in account. Far from getting the account audited, parties went all the way to camouflage the whole matter. Several Congress leaders took pride in the manner in which Sita Ram Kesari was managing the account. They quote—*No books, no accounts, whatever Kesari does is real account.*

Lack of inner democracy in the political parties is another major drawback which has been casting its shadow on our entire political set up since long. Members find no outlet to air their views in free and frank manner. They have to think ten times from the leadership. They are, in fact, subservient to the will and wishes of the leaders and have no option but to toe their lines. To remain and continue to survive in politics is several times more difficult than joining politics. The survival instinct makes the members meek and submissive. With the result leaders of political parties take their members for granted. These were some of the reasons on the basis of which Jayaprakash Narayan propagated the idea of "partyless democracy" to completely transform our entire political set up. Some of the parties have reduced themselves to be nothing more than fief of their leaders. Organisational elections do not take place for decades together. A leadership which throttles democracy within the party and does not allow others to increase their political weight can not contribute to the making and building of political institutions in accordance with the democratic norms. Parties like BSP, Indian National Lok Dal, AIADMK and Samajwadi Party, etc. are thriving on the basis of personality cult without promoting or accommodating as its working is not in conformity with the ideals for which it has hitherto been known. Though it calls itself an umbrella organization representing all walks of life and people from all different groups and community, it is nevertheless under the clutch and grips of its leadership drawn from Nehru dynasty.

The Congress which never secured more than 45 per cent votes except in 1957 and 1984 General elections, ruled this country at center as well as in large number of States. A vast difference between percentage of seats obtained by parties would make it easier to understand that the present election system has been favourable to Congress party in several ways. In 1952 General elections, the party secured only 45 per cent votes and managed to bag 74.5 per cent of the Lok Sabha seats. The will of the sovereign people is not reflected in the legislatures. Sometimes the will of the people is distorted and diluted by the ruling party having minority votes. Congress formed government in 1984 with 415 seats but it had not secured even half of the total valid votes cast. In spite of 52 per cent voters not voting in favour of Congress, it was able to secure more than two-thirds majority in the Lok Sabha. While its vote share was only 48.12 per cent, it could secure 76 per cent of seats. Similarly, V.P. Singh in 1989 got only 17.66 per cent votes but got 27 per cent seats in Lok Sabha. Likewise Janata Government in 1977 secured 296 seats in Lok Sabha but polled 43 per cent votes cast. For the last 50 years, India has been governed by a minority votes. Indian historian Ramchandra Guha in the book *Indira after Gandhi* argues that the country is only "50 per cent democracy", holding viable election, but falling short when it comes to the functioning of politicians and politician institutions.

An indepth study of elections to State assemblies would show the same position. Even in the Lok Sabha elections held in 2004, about 60 percent MPs could get less than half of the total votes polled. They were elected because of division of votes among different parties and candidates. It was this single most serious flaw in our electoral system which helped Congress to perpetuate its rule for 40 years with features of one Party Dominance having one party rule in States and at the Centre.

Constitutional expert Ivor Jennings too was skeptical about experimenting Westminster model of parliamentary system in India. He remarked that this system is surviving in Britain because of two-party system there. If these two parties fragment into several parties as happen in India, the parliamentary system can not survive in Britain. Dr. R. Venkataraman, former President of India, while delivering lecture at India International Centre on 16th October 1999 said that in 1965 he had fired first salvo against Parliamentary form by sending a Resolution to AICC asking for the constitution of a Committee to examine and report—"Whether the present form of Government at the Centre and the States may be replaced by an executive directly elected by the people for a fixed term of years and if so to recommend the consequential changes in the constitution of India as appropriate." He was critical of the declining trends emerging in parliamentary system in India and had openly suggested for a system where an amalgamation of executive and parliament each organ exercising their sovereign powers with checks and balance.

Recognition of Political Parties—Some Aspects

Working of political parties in India is distinguished by its features of multiplicity with preponderance of small regional parties. Neither Constitution nor Representation of Peoples Act 1951 imposes any stringent condition for forming a political party and getting its registered. It makes no provision with regard to recognition. Section 29A of the Act permits any association or body of individual citizens of India calling itself a political party to make an application to the Election Commission for seeking its registration as political party. Application must contain specific provision that the association or body shall bear true faith and allegiance to the Constitution of India as by law established and to the principles of socialism, secularism and democracy and would uphold the sovereignty, unity and integrity of India. With such liberal provisions, it is quite obvious that task of forming a political party and get it registered is not difficult. This has resulted in registration of more than 550 political parties. If a party is recognized in four or more states it is declared as National Party. The number of National parties has been varying from 14 to 7 owing to continuous review of the status based on the performance of the parties. In 1951 there were 14 National parties while presently there are 7 such parties. The number of National parties was four in year 1957, 8 in 1971, 5 in 1977, 6 in 1980, 7 in 1984, 8 in 1989, 9 in 1991, 8 in 1996, 7 in 1998 and 1999.

As per Election Symbols (Reservations and Allotment) Order 1968 only a registered political party can seek recognition. As per Section 6A of the Order, a political party shall be treated as a recognized National party, if and only if—either (A) (i) the candidates set up by it, in any four or more States, at the last general election to the House of the People, or to the Legislative Assembly of the State concerned have secured not less than six per cent of the total valid votes polled in their respective states at that general election and (ii) in addition, it has returned at least four members to the House of the People at the aforesaid last general election from any State or States. Or B (i) its candidates have been elected to the House of the people at the last general election to that House, from at least two per cent of the total number of parliamentary constituencies in India, any fraction exceeding one half being counted as one and (ii) the said candidates have been elected to that House from not less than three states. For recognition of a State party Section 6(B) provides that a political party shall be treated as a recognized state party in a state if and only if either (A) (i) the candidates set up by it at the last general election to the House of the People or to the Legislative Assembly of the State concerned have secured not less than six per cent for the total votes polled in that State and (ii) in addition it has returned at least two members to the Legislative Assembly of the State at the last general election to that Assembly or (B) it wins at least three per cent of the total number of seats in the Legislative Assembly of the State or at least three seats in the Assembly whichever is more at the general election. The aforesaid order and the criteria for recognition does not contain any provision about the audit of account, inner democracy or any violation of code of conduct in election or violation of the mandatory provisions as laid down under Section 29A of the Representative of Peoples Act 1951. No action has so far been taken to de-recognise a political party if it founds indulging in acts of violating norms of social harmony necessary for free and fair election in the country. Election Commission has on a number of occasions warned the parties, issued notices and held the political parties responsible for acts of irregularity. But it has so far refrained from taking a drastic action in the absence of effective law, rules and directives. Hence, it has become imperative that necessary amendments are introduced in the Election Symbols (Reservations and Allotment) Order 1968 to incorporate additional provisions for withdrawing the recognition in the event of any political party found indulged in corrupt practices, violating the norms of unity, integrity and social harmony of the country or indulging in misuse of official machinery or un-ethical activities.

Benefits of recognition which include certain privileges such as access to electoral rolls, provision of time for political broadcasts on the state-owned television and radio stations, Doordarshan and also the allocation of party symbols, etc. can be withdrawn from a political party which has not got its accounts duly audited or in case it is found collecting money from dubious sources in a clandestine manner or indulging in any corrupt practice. Certain stringent measures as suggested by National Commission to Review the Constitution can be considered relating to a political party under Section 29A of the Representation of Peoples Act of 1951. As per Para 6A of the Order, a political party shall be treated as a recognized National Party, only if either (A) (i) the candidates set up by it, in any four or more States, at the last general election to the House of the People, or to the Legislative Assembly of the State concerned, have secured not less than six per cent of the total valid votes polled in their respective States at that general election, and (ii) in addition, it has returned at least four members to the House of the People at the aforesaid last general election from any State or States. Or (B) (i) its candidates have been elected to the House of the People, at the last general election in that House, from at least two per cent of the total number of parliamentary constituencies in India, any fraction exceeding one-half being counted as one; and (ii) the said candidates have been elected to that House from not less than three States.

A political party, other than a National Party shall be treated as a recognized State party in a State or States, only if either the candidates set up by it, at the last general election to the House of the People, or to the Legislative Assembly of the State concerned, have secured not less than six per cent of the total valid votes polled in that State at that general election and (ii) in addition, it has returned at least two members to the Legislative Assembly of the State at the last general election to that Assembly. Or it wins at least three per cent of the total number of seats in the Legislative Assembly of the State (any fraction exceeding one-half being counted as one), or at least three seats in the Assembly, whichever is more at the aforesaid general election. The question whether a political party so recognized after any subsequent general election to the House of the People or, as the case may be, to the Legislative Assembly of the State concerned, shall be dependent upon the fulfillment by it of the conditions specified in the said paragraphs on the result of that general elections.

The Election Symbols Order does not confer any specific privilege or preference to a recognized political party except that it has acquired recognition for scrupulously adhering to the laid down objectives and is capable to gradually expand its base amongst the electorate. Granting privilege or preference on the ground of recognition in any form or manner would have offended those political parties which were at a nascent stage and just formed to spread their wings. While the recognition can "be withdrawn at the discretion of the Election Commission after giving notice, it can not de-register a political party except when it is found that a party has obtained registration through fraudulent means, or it is declared by the Government as unlawful. The Commission can also de-register if the party itself intimated the Commission that it had ceased to function or had changed its party constitution or that it would not be possible for it to function according to law.

Use of Religion, Caste and Regional Sentiments by the Political Parties

To further political prospects, parties use emotive issues based on religion, caste and regional aspirations. The influence of these issues on elections and decision-making process has been so overwhelming that several parties have openly declared their allegiance and named their parties after religion. Parties like Muslim League, Hindu Mahasabha, Ram Rajya Parishad, Akali Dal, Shiv Sena, etc. are the parties which have unequivocally declared their allegiance to the religions they preach and profess. Muslim League was the first political party formed in the name of religion in 1906 paving the way for other parties to come up on the political map. Several non-political organizations like Rashtriya Swayamsevak Sangh and Vishwa Hindu Parishad, etc. came into existence to act as pressure groups to influence political events without directly joining the political activities. Though these organizations do not proclaim themselves to be political parties with any political ambition, nevertheless they had dominated the political events at both centre and state levels by providing ideological and other logistic support to political parties.

Congress, though claim to be a secular party, has not remained behind in exploiting religious sentiments for political purposes. While it has always raised the bogey of communalism as biggest threat to the country's integrity, it has been practising policy of appeasement towards minorities particularly Muslims since independence. It had formed electoral alliances with parties which have been known for their communal activities. While it had blamed and targeted the Hindu organizations like RSS and others for every communal riot without verifying the facts, its stand against organizations like Jamat-i-Islami, Muslim League and others has never been vocal even in the face of availability of evidences and inquiry reports. Considering minorities as its vote banks, it overtly and covertly allowed illegal migrants from neighbouring countries particularly Bangladesh to settle down in the country and regularized their settlement by issuing Food Cards and other proofs of residence. Its act of getting through the Illegal Migrants—Determination by Tribunal Act 1983 could speak the volumes of its concern to consolidate vote banks amongst minorities. Its stand on Supreme Court's judgment in case of Shahbano and its subversion through amendment in the law would make it suffice to prick needle in its secular balloon. Its act of providing five per cent reservation to Muslims in government jobs in Andhra Pradesh, extending reservations for Muslims in Aligarh Muslim University beyond 50 per cent and its role in the course of Supreme Court judgments in the past will provide enough grounds to un-earth its bogey of secularism. It was this no-holds-barred appeasement of minorities by Congress which led other political parties like Bhartiya Janata Party to find some emotive issues to counter as an electoral move. It openly came out for the revival of ancient Indian Culture and regarded Hinduism as way of life and an essential attribute of nationalism. The mishandling of Ayodhya issue and opening of Ramjanm Bhoomi for worship by the Congress led Government provided this party as an effective tool to win support of majority of the people.

The issue of reservation on religious grounds, which has come in the wake of decision of Andhra Pradesh Government, has now added new dimensions to the whole electoral politics. Similar demands have started coming up in other States. The Uttar Pradesh Government has recently assured the Muslims for extending reservation in government jobs to them in the same manner as done by Andhra Government. The Central Government has gone to the extent of considering amendment in the Constitution. Such a move would however go against the wishes of the framers of the Constitution. A study of the debates in the Constituent Assembly would reveal that members were unanimous in dispensing with any move to incorporate reservation on religious grounds. Taking cognizance of the gravity of the issue, Constituent Assembly had formed an *Advisory Committee on Minorities* comprising 40 members including Muslims under the Chairmanship of Sardar Patel. The Committee did painstaking work and deliberated the matter thoroughly. However, it came to the conclusion that the very idea of introducing reservation on religious or on minority grounds is fraught with serious consequences. The Committee concluded that the time has come when the minority communities have themselves realized after great reflection the evil effects in the past of such reservation on the minorities themselves, and the reservations should be dropped. In a House of about 40 members of the Advisory Committee, there was only one solitary vote against the proposal and 39 members voted for the burial of this explosive issue once for all. Delivering his speech in the Constituent Assembly, Sardar Patel said: "enough consideration was given to consult proposals from minority communities including Muslims. If they really have come to the conclusion that in the changed conditions of this country, it is in the interest of all to lay down real and genuine foundation of a secular State, then nothing is better for the minorities than to trust the good-sense and sense of fairness of the majority and to place confidence in them. But in the long run, it would be in the interest of all to forget that there is anything like majority or minority in this country and that in India there is only one community known as Indians." These words drew such a tremendous response that all the Muslim members supported the motion for withdrawal of reservation on religious or minority grounds. Dr. Ambedkar, however, took a different stand altogether by describing the majority community as 'communal' and minorities as 'explosive force'. His views that minorities being 'explosive force' can blow up the whole fabric of the state drew flak from all the members of the Assembly. Shri L. Krishnaswamy Bharathi, an active member of the Assembly criticized Ambedkar in these words: "Dr. Ambedkar says that the minorities have loyally accepted the rule of the majority which is basically a communal majority and not a political majority. I do not know what he has at the back of his mind. There was only one party which functioned on the political plane, the Indian National Congress, which was entirely a non-communal organization and a political party. And yet Dr. Ambedkar says it is basically a 'communal majority' which is not true in fact. I must say it is wrong, mischievous and misleading."

Our Constitution makes no provision for reservation on grounds of religion. A conjoint reading of Article 15 and Article 16 makes it amply clear that it creates a bar against any move to introduce reservation on the ground of religion. Article 15 lays down that the State shall not discriminate against any citizen on grounds only of religion, race, caste, sex, place of birth or any of them. Article 16 states that there shall be equality of opportunity for all citizens in matters relating to employment or appointment to any office under the State. In the case of *Triloki Nath Tiku & Ors* vs. *State of Jammu and Kashmir and Others AIR 1969 SC*, Supreme Court held the 50 per cent reservation for posts of Muslims by the Government of Jammu and Kashmir as unconstitutional. On the matter relating to reservation of appointments for "backward classes", it held that the members of an entire caste or community may in the social, economic and educational scale of values at a given time be backward and may on that account be treated as backward class, but that is not because they are members of a community but because they form a class. For the purpose of Article 16(4) in determining whether a section forms a class, a test solely based on caste, community, race, religion, sex, descent, place of birth or residence can not be adopted because it would directly offend the Constitution.

The political parties in India face organizational problems in regard to discipline, defections, intra-party organizations, elections within the parties, and splits in the party. Raising of adequate funds for party organizations and activities by legitimate means and their appropriate and effective utilization during non-election and election periods is a perennial problem, criminalisation of politics and politicization of criminals and the maintenance of public ethics is another area of concern in respect of party functioning.

Areas of Reform: Thus in the perspective of the evolution of political parties in India during the last 50 years as described, some of the areas of reform have been suggested from time to time at different levels by experts, committees, etc. which should be of immediate concern:

1. Institutionalization of Political Parties—Need for a Comprehensive Legislation to regulate party activities. Criteria for registration as a national or State party—de-recognition of parties.
2. Structural and Organizational Reforms—Party organizations—national, State and local levels—inner party democracy—regular party elections, recruitment of party cadres, socialization, development and training, research, thinking and policy planning activities of the party.
3. Problems of Party Funding—Need for a Legislation to regulate party funds—distribution and spending of party funds during non-election and election times.
4. Maintenance of Regular Accounts by the Political Parties—Auditing and publishing—making audited accounts available for open inspection.
5. Party System and Electoral System—To what extent and in what way the electoral system could be reformed so as to pave the way for the establishment of stable governments based on the concept of two party system or dual party alliance system—Do we need to change the system of single member constituencies to a mixed system or a proportional method of representation along with the simple majority system?
6. Steps to check criminalisation of political parties.
7. Steps to curb the role of casteism and communalism.
8. Problem of proliferation of independent candidates.
9. Strengthening of Anti-Defection Measures—Amendments in Law.

10. Party System and Governance—How to make parties as viable instruments for good governance?
11. Restoration of values and morality in public life.

A number of academic and research institutions, political observers and analysts, committees and commissions appointed by the Government of India from time to time and concerned scholars, journalists and academicians in their individual capacities have made a number of proposals for reforms in the party system in India. Some of the most significant of these are culled here in order to provide a perspective for framing recommendations for party reforms.

Political parties should ensure that criminals are denied tickets for elections. Entry of criminals can be prevented without passing any law. It is within the powers of the political parties to see that no criminal or people with the reputation of being in criminal activities are selected as candidates. There is no need for any amendment in People's Representation Act or in the Constitution for that. Anti-Defection Law, under which one-third members of the total strength of a party are allowed to split it, is not working well. If anybody wants to change his party after being elected on that party's ticket, he should resign from Parliament or the Legislature and face electorate. If there is a rule like that, may be very few defections will take place.

1. Reforming the first-past-the-post system of election. The German model that accepts a preferential voting system can be examined for insuring proportionate representation of parties in parliament.
2. Since all parties work in tandem with unscrupulous business lobbies and gangsters or use state power for determining the outcome of elections, these cancerous trends need to be checked for good governance.
3. Political parties should have minimum principles for forming a coalition government rather than forge alliances only to be in government. Unprincipled political alignment should be discouraged by law urging political parties to be more homogenous in

their joint endeavours of running the coalition government.

4. Support to be rendered to any government from "outside", i.e. without joining the coalition government, should be legally barred. Only a party having at least 25 per cent seats in the Lower House of parliament or Assembly should have a chance to form the government.
5. No government should be removed from office if the opposition parties or others involved in the toppling game fail to come out with a clear alternative arrangement and programme.
6. The kind of coalitional arrangements that the parties make should be clear before forming the government. Developments so far show that the big parties themselves prefer to play second fiddle to the regional and smaller parties whose immediate interests are determined by 'regional and parochial' issues rather than long term national programmes.
7. Parties need to strengthen their managerial and crisis management capacity. If the party organizations are better managed and democratized, their efficiency would increase. More autonomy to all layers and more inner-party democracy would help circulate leaders on the basis of their qualities. The criterion of achievement rather than ascription should be accepted by all parties. Unless parties are broad based in accommodating all segments of society, they continue to become status quoist, exclusivist, regional and sectarian.
8. Parties' own code of conduct and self-initiated reforms, rather than state imposed reforms are likely to improve the working of parties.

Parties Dependence on Caste Based Politics

The caste system, which has hitherto been a social factor finding its mythological basis from the concept of *Varnashram,* has been used by political parties to further their electoral prospects. Since every constituency has combinations voters belonging to different castes, a political party is bound to keep its tabs on caste equations while putting up its candidate for election. Apart from making caste appeals at constituency level, several political parties have adopted policy—approach to woo the voters belonging to different castes such as Scheduled Castes, Scheduled Tribes, Dalits and Other Backward Classes by promising good working and living conditions through reservation in job and freedom from atrocities from the higher castes. All sorts of practices, fair or foul, are adopted to tilt the caste equations in favour of their candidates. While at constituencies level, parties would even put up two dummy candidates belonging to same caste with a view to divide votes, they will have no qualms in issuing sentimental appeals to change the caste equations at a national or state level to prove their credentials. The extension of reservation in government jobs for SC/ST candidates was extended after every ten years.

When the caste based appeal assume significance in an election, the merit and qualitative background of the candidates takes backseat. A person is elected merely because he comes from a group of people predominantly belonging to a particular caste. Once elected, he has no option but to act as an appendage of that group and promotes the interests of the people belonging to the caste so as to vindicate his election. This phenomenon unleashes a chain reaction to systematically erode the fabric of our polity. This caste based politics which dominates the electoral ballots particularly in U.P., Bihar and Haryana has sent mediocre as representatives who were unable to contribute anything good for the governance.

As the caste-considerations have become decisive factors for all political parties while putting up candidates, no fool-proof system can be devised to curb this practice. No provision has been made in the Representation of the Peoples Act 1951 to curb the caste appeals during elections effectively. Section 123(3)A merely says that it will amount to "corrupt practice" to attempt to promote feelings of enmity or hatred between different classes of the citizens of India on the grounds of religion, race, caste, community or language, by a candidate or his agent or any other person for the furtherance of the prospects of the election of that candidate. This provision covers only the attempt to promote feeling of enmity or hatred. It does not cover the attempts to woo voters on caste appeals. In U.P. Assembly elections, BSP gave slogan—*"Tilak, Taraju or Talwar, Inko maro joote char"*. The message contained in this slogan was clear—Brahmins (Tilak), Vaishya (Taraju) and Kshatriya (Talwar) should be beaten up with shoes. Now if we apply Section 123(3)A, this slogan undoubtedly falls within the sweep of "attempt to promote feeling of enmity or hatred". The slogan is obviously an attempt to promote feeling of enmity and it was raised in public meetings wherever BSP leaders addressed. Yet no action was taken. This establishes the infirmity not only in our political system but also of our legal system which could not bring such a clear inciting slogan within the sweep of "Corrupt Practice". No election was declared null and void in spite of existence of all evidences and press reports.

It is worthwhile to mention that caste based politics finds its roots in the policy of reservation of seats in schools, colleges and also in government jobs. In Assembly elections 2003, Congress Governments in Rajasthan and Haryana extended reservations to Jats, who were otherwise never listed as other Backward Castes. The move was wholly political and an attempt to win Jat votes by luring them with the goodies of reservation.

One of the worst form of caste based politics which attracted the attention from world all over was reflected in the agitation in 1990 over Mandal Commission Report. The Report was submitted to the government in 1988 but no government considered it for implementation. Shri V.P. Singh the then Prime Minister introduced the report and took all necessary steps for its implementation. During his Prime Ministership, Shri V.P. Singh wanted to strengthen his position and acquire a charisma at least among the backward classes which were hitherto the vote banks of Congress Party. His attempt was likened to killing two birds with one stone. At that time Shri Devi Lal was the Deputy Prime Minister and his influence in the government as well as politics at the centre was growing. He was regarded as the scion of the jat dominated northern belt. Shri V.P. Singh was, therefore, badly in search of an issue which could serve his multiple aims. Obviously, no other issue except the Mandal Commission Report could have been a better choice under the given volatile situation. The implementation of the Report evoked sharp reactions from amongst the masses in general and youths in particular. The whole country was plunged in month long agitation. Never before and not even during freedom struggle, students took the extreme step of burning themselves hitting headlines world over. While presenting the Mandal Commission Report before Parliament, Shri Singh had himself stated that there were about 52 per cent people falling under the category of "Other Backward Classes". In contrast to this enormous population, hardly one per cent population of the country was in government job. So it is quite obvious that by mere reservation of few posts in government service, we can not provide relief and succour to the backward classes which constitute 52 per cent of the total population.

The fact that caste-based politics will continue to haunt the Indian political system with all its ill adverse effects has made it imperative for the political pundits, constitutionalists and intellectuals to find out some workable solution to save our institutions from falling into the state of deterioration. The measures which can be introduced to discourage the bane of casteism from corrupting our institutions can be summed up as under:

- Representation of Peoples Act 1951 should be amended to provide disqualifications for candidates if they are found referring to castes in any form or manner during their election campaign. It should be clearly brought within the purview of corrupt practice as defined under Section 123.
- Election Manifesto, posters, banners and pamphalets, etc. should not contain any appeal or promise or

reference which directly or indirectly tend to promote caste-related feelings.

- Persons found encouraging caste appeals during elections should be deprived of their right of franchise for three to five years.
- No political party finding its roots on caste based politics should be granted registration. If any registered political party is found promoting casteism, its registration should be kept under suspension till remedial actions are taken by it.
- Reservation on the basis of caste or religion should be kept away from electoral practices.
- Code of conduct for political parties needs to be given a re-look to add deterrent provision to put a curb on activities relating to caste.

The fact can not be disputed that in case the Presidential form of government is introduced, the whole country is one constituency and there is absolutely no reason for any candidate for Presidency that he will make caste appeals. Whereas in Parliamentary system, MPs are elected from smaller constituencies where narrow appeals on castes can affect the election results. Perhaps no other reform or measure except the Presidential form of government can better checkmate the caste-based politics.

8

Constraints in the Working of Coalition

Formation of coalition governments on the basis of pre-poll or post-poll alliances of different political parties has come to stay as essential feature of Indian Political system. For sharing power, parties were seen sacrificing their cherished ideals and taking sides under what they call "Common Minimum Programme". The regional political parties which had hitherto confined their roles and activities to their respective States or regions, have now come to play decisive roles in formation of governments at the Centre. Their role at the Centre had been found more commendable than the roles they had so far been playing in their states. The political events took place during the last few years have demonstrated that political parties, in spite of their inherent contradictions, can play decisive roles with sense of accountability. Nevertheless, it would be an exaggeration to say that coalition politics is free from constraints. These include difficulties in sharing power, political rivalries, bickerings, use of black money, misuse of Constitutional provisions such as Article 356 by the Government at the Centre to either topple a government or prevent an alliance from forming the governments, defections and all sorts of machinations to create or find out some issue to pull down or embarrass the government. Clouds of instability remain in sight with all their consequences. In fact it is the multiplicity of political parties which is at the root of the whole problem. Harold J. Laski, author of *Parliamentary Government in England* laid emphasis on the maximum of two parties. He expounded a rule that for any parliamentary system to run successfully, two and only two parties must be in the fray. Any increase in population of political parties is bound to throw the whole system out of gear.

In retrospect, coalition politics is not new to Indian political system. Under Government of India Act 1935, coalition governments had worked in several provinces. The dawn of independence, however, saw new scenario developing on political horizon of the country. It marked the beginning of one party dominance which continued to hold its sway all over the country for nearly 20 years. The general elections in 1967 marked the beginning of a new era in political set up of the country. It saw the downfall of one party dominance. In as many as nine States, Congress was ousted from power. However, inability of any party getting clear majority on its own raised apprehensions about survival of governments formed by coalition of political parties. These apprehensions were compounded further due to poking of nose in every political event of the States by the Congress led government at Centre. E.M.S. Namboodripad, a known Communist leader once remarked that unless the States were given maximum authority, there was "every likelihood of Bangladesh repeated in India."

Experiments of Coalition Governments at the Centre

The experience of forming a coalition government at the Centre can be traced to the year 1977 when several opposition parties joined together to form a government headed by Morarji Desai. The experiment, however, could not last more than half of the term. Congress offered its unconditional support to Chaudhary Charan Singh, the then Home Minister in Morarji Government, for his becoming Prime Minister. The idea was to pull down the government and install a puppet regime to survive at the wishes of the Congress. This caused ripple in the whole coalition and Morarji had to resign without completing his term. As the aim of the Congress was to somehow crack the coalition, it subsequently withdrew its support from Chaudhary Charan Singh and thereby paved the way for election. The country underwent a sort of political crisis with instability as its hallmark. The Congress, taking advantage of the volatile political situation raised slogan "Elect that Government that works" and staged a comeback in 1980 mid-term elections. The first ever experiment at the Centre thus went nosedived.

The country witnessed the same political scenario in 1989 when Congress, headed by Rajiv Gandhi was ousted from power and a coalition government headed by V.P. Singh took over the reigns. The experiment of coalition, however, once again failed the country when as a response to his Mandal Commission Card, BJP took up the Ayodhya issue and carried out a Rath Yatra. Shri L.K. Advani was detained providing a cause for withdrawing the support from the coalition government. Congress was at it once again. It tactically chose to support Chander Shekhar as Prime Minister and subsequently withdrew its support within less than three months of his becoming Prime Minister. The trivial allegation that two policemen from Haryana were doing secret surveillance of the residence of Shri Rajiv Gandhi was made a ground to withdraw the support. Thus the second experiment of coalition government at the Centre failed the country again. People finding no solution to their problems and stability at the Centre, had to remain disillusioned.

The year 1991 saw the horizon of new political trends when in General Elections to Lok Sabha, Congress emerged as the largest party and chose Narasimha Rao to become Prime Minister. It, however, lacked full majority. Getting wind of the vulnerability of nine MPs belonging to Jharkhand Mukti Morcha, it managed to secure their support by all means fair or foul. To enlist their support, JMM MPs were paid hefty bribes running into crores of rupees besides luxurious vehicles and flats in Delhi's posh areas just days before the Lok Sabha took up no-confidence motion on July 29, 1993. The then Union Ministers Buta Singh, Capt. Satish Sharma and Ajit Singh and Bhajan Lal and Veerappa Moily former Chief Ministers of Haryana and Karnataka respectively were booked and chargesheeted by the CBI. Former Karnataka Minister N.H. Revanna and Rama Linga Reddy, former Rajya Sabha

MP Rajeshwar Rao and Bangalore based liquor barrons D.K. Adikesavulu and Mr. Thimme Gowda were other names which figured in the whole game. Sufficient evidences were furnished during trial which included joint and individual accounts of Suraj Mandal, Shibu Soren, Simon Marandi and Shailendra Mahato having deposits totaling over to Rs. 20 million in the Punjab National Bank in New Delhi. The fact that vehicles were made available to them just three days before the date of no-confidence motion was also proved. Shailendra Mahato MP had turned approver in the case. All the JMM MPs were detained and remanded for thorough investigation. However, Narasimha Rao, Bhajan Lal and Moily filed Special Leave Petition in Supreme Court seeking constitutional immunity under Article 105 of the Constitution.

Article 105(2) of the Constitution grants an immunity to Members of Parliament for their acts associated with the work of Parliament or its Committees. It lays down—No member of Parliament shall be liable to any proceedings in any Court in respect of anything said or any vote given by him in Parliament or any Committee thereof, and no person shall be so liable in respect of the publication by or under the authority of either House of Parliament or any paper, report, notes or proceedings. The Supreme Court, on the ground of this Constitutional immunity discharged nine former MPs including Suraj Mandal, Soren and Marandi of the JMM. The court ruled that they could not be tried in the case as they enjoyed immunity from prosecution for voting inside Parliament under Article 105 of the Constitution.

In spite of the MPs getting relief under the Constitutional immunity and other technical grounds, the fact that money had changed hands and corrupt practice was adopted to save the government, left deep scar on the already crumbling edifice of political system. The fact that money and manipulations have carved a deep niche in our political system found its manifestation in several subsequent events. The recent *Cash-for-query scam* 2005 which took the toll of membership of 11 MPs gives a vivid description of stinking and dwindling political system. It has forced all political analysts, thinkers and

Constitutional experts to find out ways and means to salvage the system and restore credibility to it.

The 1996 General Elections added further impetus to the deteriorating political scenario in the country. In the elections, no party could get majority. Since Bhartiya Janata Party had emerged as the single largest Party, President Shankar Dayal Sharma, following past precedents, invited its leader Atal Behari Vajpayee to form the government. The Government, however, could not last beyond 13 days as he had to tender resignation just at the nick of trial of strength on the floor of Lok Sabha. The Congress supported H.D. Deve Gowda to head the United Front Government. Pursuing the same tricks of trade, Congress withdrew its support from Deve Gowda and his United Front Government on the vague and specious plea that it has no faith in his leadership and pressed for new leader. On April 11, 1997, the 10 Month old government was voted out of power in the Lok Sabha. The country was thus again dragged into a state of political instability wherein talks of fresh election filled the air. The political expediency forced both the United Front and the Congress to avoid election as neither was in a position to face the polls and provide BJP an opportunity to improve its tally. As a result, Shri Inder Kumar Gujral was chosen to head the coalition government and was sworn in as third Prime Minister within two years since 1996 General Elections.

However, the Congress was restive and unwilling to continue its support to Gujral Government either. Its constant search for some plausible ground to withdraw support bore fruit when Jain Commission inquiring into the assassination of Rajiv Gandhi submitted its interim report indicting DMK's role. Congress raised a full-throated controversy and demanded the resignation of DMK ministers in Gujral's Council of Ministers. Gujral, however, rejected the demand outrightly. Congress explored every possibility to form its Government enlisting support of constituents of United Front. Finding this proposition as costlier and self-defeating, it finally chose to repeat its past tricks of withdrawing support yet again. After four days of deliberations, Congress Working

Committee finally decided "unanimously" to pull the rags and bring down the barely seven months old Gujral Government. Congress President Sita Ram Kesari met the President K.R. Narayanan and informed him of his party's decision to withdraw support and staked a claim to form a new government. In his letter to the President, Kesari asked K.R. Narayanan to explore the possibilities of forming an alternative government without resorting to dissolution of the House. He even assured him that given the chance Congress would be able to prove majority on the floor of the House. An hour after the Congress withdrew support to the United Front Government, Prime Minister I.K. Gujral submitted his resignation to the President. President accepted resignation, dissolved the Lok Sabha and ordered for elections. These events ultimately shattered the commonman's faith in the working of coalition governments.

The Mid-Term-Poll 1998 returned a hung Lok Sabha yet again. Though BJP improved its tally and had forged a pre-poll alliance, yet the completion of five year term was in doubt. Atal Behari Vajpayee was once again sworn in as Prime Minister. However, sick of AIADMK's demand for its pound of flesh and its leader Jayalalitha's tough posturing proved a major setback so much that in spite of capable leadership provided by Vajpayee, the Government could not last beyond 13 months. In a trial of strength, Vajpayee Government lost vote of confidence by one vote. Had its MP GMC Balyogi, who was Speaker, could be counted, the Government would have survived. President Narayanan gave ample opportunity to Sonia Gandhi to muster support and reach to the magic figure of 272. Finding no option, he ordered dissolution of Lok Sabha and sent the country to mid-term-poll. Another aspect which has hitherto penetrated the minds of political thinkers relates to the feasibility of bringing no-confidence motion without preparing for providing an effective alternative. The dictum—you should not demolish a thing which you can not build remained the talk of town. Behind the curtain political events led to the end of yet another coalition experiment at the Centre.

The year 1999 will go down in the annals of India's political system as the most remarkable year as it was in this year that country saw emergence of new political equation. Never before country saw any coalition government with 24 political parties to last its full term. In the General Elections held in September 1999, the pre-poll alliance under the banner of National Democratic Alliance and popular leadership provided by Atal Behari Vajpayee swept the polls, got clear majority and formed the government to complete its full term and played a key role in country's all round progress.

In General Elections 2004, the electorate returned a hung Lok Sabha yet again. The ruling National Democratic Alliance could not come back to power. Congress with 145 members emerged as single largest party but was far away from the decisive mark of 272 members. With this figure, it had no option but forge an alliance and claim to form government. The country witnessed a sort of political upheaval when a post-poll alliance was formed comprising political parties such as Congress (145 MPs), DMK (16), Nationalist Congress Party (9), Telangana Rajya Samiti (5), PMK (6), MDMK (4), RJD (21), JMM (5), Lok Janshakti Party (4), JK PDP (1), CPI(M) (43), CPI (12), SP (36), and JD(S) (3). Headed by Smt. Sonia Gandhi, the alliance was named as United Progressive Alliance (UPA). When President Abdul Kalam invited the leader of UPA, Mrs. Sonia Gandhi to form government, she declined in the wake of call of nation wide protest from BJP firebrand Mrs. Sushma Swaraj and Ms. Uma Bharti. For nearly a week, country remained under grip of unprecedented leadership vaccum as UPA remained indecisive. Political parties and Congress leaders flocked to 10 Janpath pressing hard for seeking reversal of stand from Mrs. Gandhi. One MP Ganga Charan Rajput went to the extent of pulling out revolver and shoot himself in full view of press and political workers present there. A big contingent of Congress workers slept on the roadside pavements to give a symbolic message and lend support to efforts seeking reversal of her stand. If we refer to her stance taken in 1999, we found her staking claim for power herself and sought one week more from the then

President K.R. Narayanan to muster the requisite strength of 272 MPs. Now for what reasons she changed her decision dramatically when she was almost certain to reach to the top slot were never made clear. Congress left with no option but to choose Dr. Manmohan Singh, former Reserve Bank Governor and later Finance Minister in Narasimha Rao Government to become country's 14th Prime Minister. Having no political experience at all, Dr. Manmohan Singh, has been known for his grip on economic and financial matters as also for his personal integrity. Smt. Sonia Gandhi, in her capacity as Chairperson of National Advisory Council has retained vast powers with her and there is nothing which is beyond her sweep. She is also the Chairperson of UPA and thus every decision relating to political affairs is to be taken by her. At one occasion, she was regarded as one of the Top Ten powerful women in the world. Finding a cue, opposition often alleged that country is having three centres of power, i.e. PM, CPM and SPM. (PM-Prime Minister), (CPM-Communist Party Marxist) and (SPM-Super Prime Minister). Often Dr. Singh is described as *De jure* Prime Minister and Smt. Gandhi as *De facto* Prime Minister. Such a position is unprecedented as the country had never before faced such a complex phenomenon. The General Election held in 2009 for 15th Lok Sabha, UPA once again came to power making it quite clear that coalition era has come to stay in Indian politics notwithstanding its infirmities and shortcomings.

An indepth study of the working of coalition government at the Centre for the entire period spanning from 1989 onwards would led us to a fair conclusion that Congress, in spite of being the old political party has never played its role as a responsible political force. Having tasted power, its leaders have never been able to resist temptation. It has developed a sort of culture around it wherein sycophancy prevails over self-respect, loyalty over capability and manipulation over integrity. Subsequent events such as Volcker Committee Report, Mitrokhin's reference to KGB distributing money to Congress leaders, Cash for Query Scam incidents of political skullduggery in Goa, Jharkhand and Madhya Pradesh and imposition of President's rule in Bihar at midnight hour only to prevent its adversary from forming government are some of the numerous instances to prick holes in its murky doings. Its stand on MP Local Area Development Fund of Rs. 2 crore per MP every year has also been ambivalent. In fact, it was the Congress Government headed by Narasimha Rao which commenced this scheme in 1993 as a part of his move to strengthen his political position. On a number of occasions, Supreme Court had to take a dig on the wrong doings. A case of Jharkhand can be specifically cited. When Governor Syed Sibte Razi sworn in Shibu Soren in spite of his not being able to give names of MLAs in his support, his blatantly partisan act of ignoring the claim of Arjun Munda having majority support drew flak from Press, people and the Court. Supreme Court had to intervene and advance the date of trial of strength before Assembly. Speaker of Lok Sabha Som Nath Chatterjee spoke against this verdict and took the view that Courts can not decide or interfere with the matters relating to legislatures. He convened a meeting of Presiding Officers of all Legislative Assemblies of States and give vent to his views on the issues. He, however, chose not to speak a word on the conduct of Governor.

Then came Bihar assembly elections in February 2005. With no party getting majority and Paswan's Lok Janshakti Party remained defiant on Muslim Chief Minister, political activities reached their crescendo. A pragmatic and cautious Nitish Kumar of JD(U) was able to enlist the support of several independents and breakaway group of MLAs belonging to LJP. He was about to formally claim for power. However, sensing the political fall outs, an emergency Cabinet meeting was convened by the Prime Minister at the instance of Lalu Prasad Yadav at midnight hour to take a decision for clamping emergency and dissolve Assembly under Article 356 of the Constitution. Centre was not to wait for the President to come from Moscow. A draft order was faxed, his signatures were obtained and the Assembly was dissolved the same night. This, however, came as blessing in disguise for Nitish Kumar, who in the fresh elections held in November thumping majority and came back to power. To sound music to his ears, Supreme Court declared the Presidential order issued under Article 356 as unconstitutional and act of Governor Buta Singh in recommending dissolution as partisan.

Debates on no-confidence motions

An analytical study of debates over no-confidence motions tabled before Parliament reveals an interesting story. First no-confidence motion against the government in independent India was brought about in the third Lok Sabha in 1963 (22 August 1963). Both the fourth and fifth Lok Sabhas witnessed the admission of two motions of no-confidence, which were turned down ultimately. During the tenure of the sixth Lok Sabha, two motions of no-confidence had come up before the House for discussion. One motion was rejected while the other saw an inconclusive debate because the government led by Morarji Desai, had resigned while the debate was still going on. With the exception of the 9th Lok Sabha which did not take up any no-confidence motion, 7th, 8th and 10th Lok Sabhas discussed in all seven no-confidence motions and all of them were rejected because the opposition was numerically in minority. There was no vote on the first one (1996) because the Vajpayee government resigned on its own at the end of the debate. Whenever such an occasion arose, the debates had acquired political overtones. Secondly, while moving no-confidence motion, no alternative was provided for a discussion thereon. At one occasion Shri Shiv Raj Patil of Congress, participating in the debate, himself referred to this infirmity in our system. He specifically referred to the German convention wherein it is mandatory for a member to provide alternative before tabling a motion of no-confidence. However, in India, the practice of citing alternative in the motion has not yet developed. One sentence motion—"This House expresses no-confidence in the Council of Ministers" has often been admitted for debates without simultaneous addition to the confidence that it was supposed to express as an alternative. Demand for making the condition of stating alternative in the motion as mandatory has not been debated upon.

When NDA was in power it maintained that there was an urgent need to find some constitutional means to provide stable governance for the country. It referred to the frequent elections and repeated hung Lok Sabha resulting in constant instability affecting economy and credibility of the system. BJP argued that a motion of no-confidence could only bring down a government but not throw up an alternative. The party advocated the adoption of a mechanism based on German system of a Constructive Vote of Confidence where any member who commands majority support in the Lower House could form the government irrespective of party affiliations. The idea that there must be a fixed tenure of Lok Sabha was also floated. It was conceived as an effective measure to pre-empt political parties from resorting to destabilizing games as they would then be compelled to form new alliances rather than go back to electorate for a fresh mandate. It was contended that a review of the Constitution was necessary in order to bring about these changes.

CPI and CPM, however, opposed the idea of introducing 'Constructive Vote of Confidence' based on German formula. They pointed out that the system of No-Confidence was not a procedure laid down by the Constitution. It was a mechanism developed as a part of the rules and procedures for conducting business in house. If the idea of constructive vote of confidence is introduced, it would deprive the opposition of exercising valuable opportunity to censure the government as the debates would be diverted from the criticism to formation of alternative government.

Congress and left parties also did not favour the idea of having a fixed term for the Lok Sabha on the ground that it would render the elected representatives unaccountable to citizens for the entire period of five years. The then President K.R. Narayanan threw a spanner in the works of NDA government's agenda for reform by stating (27 January 2000) that it is not the Constitution that has failed but it is we who have failed the Constitution. He also disagreed with the idea of switching over to Presidential form of government and stated that 'political instability' was not a sufficient reason to discard the parliamentary form of government.

In April 1999, when NDA government lost no-confidence by just one vote, L.K. Advani called Girdhar Gamang vote as subversion of mandate. He said that the government would have survived "if our adversaries had not taken the assistance of the Chief Minister of a State, who according to all procedures of the House, would have not been allowed to vote."

In the past, opposition had used no-confidence motion as an effective weapon to embarrass the government. On August 19, 2003 when Lok Sabha took up the No-Confidence Motion for debate, Atal Behari Vajpayee remarked—"I have seen many no-confidence motions but nothing like this. A no-trust motion is brought when a government is on the verge of collapse or to keep it on its toes. But I wonder why such a motion has been moved now when there is no question of our government breaking nor do you intend to break it." He added that two days of debate have not explained the opposition's reasons for introducing the no-confidence motion.

9

Excessive Use of Power to Issue Ordinances

President's power to issue ordinance when both the Houses of Parliament are not in session has been the subject of criticism since the first Parliament commenced its business. Article 123 of the Constitution provides that if at any time, except when both the Houses of Parliament are in session, the President is satisfied that circumstances exist which render it necessary for him to take immediate action, he may promulgate such Ordinances as the circumstances appear to him to require. Such an Ordinance has to be laid before both Houses of Parliament and shall cease to operate at the expiration of six weeks from the reassembly of Parliament. It can be issued by the President as soon as either House is prorogued. The Ordinance, if issued prior to prorogation is notified shall be void. Regarding the existence of circumstances, the satisfaction of the President is final and is not opened for any scrutiny or justiciability. It can be withdrawn at any time by the President. The Ordinance thus issued carries the same force as an Act of Parliament.

The ordinance-making power as vested in the President is unusual in a democratic Constitution for the reason that it is not to be exercised after taking people or their representatives into confidence and secondly it carries the same effect as that of law-making which is the domain of Parliament. Justifying these provisions, Dr. Ambedkar, Chairman Drafting Committee said:

> My submission to the House is that it is difficult to imagine cases where the powers conferred by the ordinary law existing at any particular moment may be deficient to deal with a situation which may suddenly and immediately arise. What is the executive to do? The executive has got a new situation arisen which it must deal with ex-hypothesi. It has not got the power to deal with that in the existing code of law. The emergency must be dealt with to promulgate the law which will enable the executive to deal with that particular situation because it cannot resort to the ordinary process of law because, again ex-hypothesi, the legislature is not in session. Therefore, it seems to me that fundamentally there is no objection to the provisions contained in Article 123.

In *R.C. Cooper* vs. *Union of India (1970) I SCC 248, 275-277,* the Supreme Court observed that the determination by the President of the existence of circumstances and the necessity to take immediate action on which the satisfaction depends, is not declared final, but expressed no opinion about the extent of the jurisdiction of the Court to examine whether the condition relating to satisfaction of the president was fulfilled. Thus the ordinances have been rendered un-justiciable in so far as the existence of circumstances and the necessity to take immediate action are concerned. So far as the constitutional validity of the provisions contained in the ordinance, it will however remain open for any judicial scrutiny.

This ordinance making provision has been so brazenly used on numerous occasions that political parties and Constitutional experts have treated the same as an affront and an anathema to the edifice of Parliamentary democracy. It is often regarded as encroachment on the powers and supremacy of the Parliament. During the 46 years from 26 January 1950 to April 1996, in all 515 Ordinances were promulgated. These include 6 Ordinances which were promulgated by the Vice President acting as President. The year 1993 saw the promulgation of maximum number of ordinances. In 1975, this power was exercised on 29 occasions. The number of Ordinances issued when the Lok Sabha was alive varies considerably. During First, Second, Third and Fourth Lok Sabha, the number of Ordinances issued was 39, 20, 31 and 34 respectively. During the Fifth Lok Sabha, i.e. from 1971 to 1977, as many as 93 Ordinances were promulgated. A close scrutiny of some of the Ordinances would reveal that these hardly require any urgency and Government could have easily waited for the session of Parliament to commence its business. Ordinances relating to financial matters having the effect of levying taxes or Excise duties, etc. do not acquire urgency to such an extent that Parliament can be deprived of discussing the implications of such orders. On several occasions, even the Constitutional Amendment ordinances were issued, e.g. the Constitution (Scheduled Tribes) Ordinance 1991. A close scrutiny of such ordinances would further reveal that they were issued as a part of rhetoric exercise to foment enthusiasm among particular segments of electorate.

It is not the opposition parties alone which have launched a tirade against the frequent promulgation of ordinances. Lok Sabha Speakers Shri G.V. Mavalankar, Shri G.S. Dhillon, Shri Balram Jakhar and President of India Dr. Shankar Dayal Sharma have from time to time opposed the growing tendency to issue ordinances. The first ever criticism to this practice came from none other than the Speaker of Lok Sabha Mr. G.V. Mavalankar who on 25th November 1950 wrote an elaborate letter to Shri Satyanaran Sinha, Minister for Parliamentary Affairs stating as follows:

> You are probably aware of the very uneasy feeling in the House over the question of the issue of Ordinances by Government from time to time. The total number of Ordinances issued so far during the course of 1950 has reached the formidable figure of 32 up to the beginning of the present session. I have neither a desire, nor am I competent to sit in judgment as to whether every one of those Ordinances was really a necessity. The Government know best the situation, and I take them as the sole and best judges thereof. I do share to some extent at

least an uneasy feeling over the issue of a very large number of Ordinances. My chief reasons are:

(i) The procedure of the issue of Ordinances is inherently undemocratic,

(ii) Whether an Ordinance is justifiable or not, the issue of a large number of Ordinances has psychologically a bad effect. The people carry an impression that the Government is carried on by Ordinances. The House carries a sense of being ignored and the Secretariat perhaps get into the habit of slackness which necessitates Ordinance and an impression is created that it is desired to commit the House to a particular legislation, as the House has no alternative, but to put its seal on matters that have been legislated upon by Ordinances.

"This feeling against Ordinances is now getting vocal in the House. Feeling that such a state of things is not conducive to the development of the best parliamentary traditions, I considered it necessary myself to look into the ten ordinances issued during the short time of about three months and I venture to give below my reactions to these for such consideration as may be deemed proper. I may say that I am addressing this to you not in any capacity as the Speaker, nor in your capacity as Minister for Parliamentary Affairs, but in my capacity as a member of the Congress Party to my colleague of the party."

However, in spite of such a strong letter coming from the Speaker of the Lok Sabha, the Government continued its practice of promulgating Ordinances under Article 123. This compelled Shri Mavalankar to write to the then Prime Minister Pt. Jawahar Lal Nehru on 17th July 1954. In his letter to the Prime Minister, Shri Mavalankar wrote as follow:

> I find in the *Times of India* of today, a news item from New Delhi dated the 16th instant, about the issue of an Ordinance to amend the Income Tax Act on the question of re-opening cases of suspected evasion. I am not writing this as regards the merits of the question. Whatever merits may be, it appears

> prima facie that, there is absolutely no urgency about the matter, and the amendments sought can be made by legislation in due course. I, therefore, write this just to apprise you of the undesirability of issuing an Ordinance for a matter of this type. The Lok Sabha is now meeting from the 23rd of August—nearly a month after—and the matter appears to be of the nature which can well wait for a month or more to enable the Lok Sabha to legislate as the Government may wish to. The Lok Sabha nowadays meets for about seven months in a year, and the inter-session period comes to about 2½ months at the most. The issue of an Ordinance is undemocratic and can not be justified, except in cases of extreme urgency or emergency.
>
> The further aspect is that we, as first Lok Sahha, carry a responsibility of laying down traditions. It is not a question of the present personnel in the Government, but a question of precedents and if this Ordinance issuing is not limited by convention, only to extreme and very urgent cases, the result may be that, in future, the Governments may go on issuing Ordinances leaving the Lok Sabha no option, but to rubber-stamp the Ordinances.

In his reply to this letter written to the Speaker on July 19, 1954, Pt. Jawahar Lal Nehru gave no assurance for putting an end to this practice. On the contrary, he defended the issuance of ordinances by saying that the Constitution itself has provided for the issue of Ordinance so how these can be considered undemocratic. He wrote in following words:

> I am myself unable to see why this should be considered undemocratic. Of course, this power, like any other power, may be abused and Parliament will be the ultimate judge as to whether the use of this power has been right or wrong. The Ordinances will of course be placed before Parliament at the earliest opportunity.

When a member questioned the feasibility of promulgating an Ordinance in the House on February 22, 1952, the Speaker Shri Mavalankar himself observed:

> I myself do not like promulgation of Ordinance. It is only in extreme cases that an Ordinance should be issued. The ordinary rule should be 'No Ordinance'.

The practice of issuing Ordinances, however, continued and all criticism from different quarters including MPs, Speaker and Constitutional experts went un-heeded. This led the then Speaker Dr. G.S. Dhillon to observe on Nov. 16, 1971 in following words:

> I agree with you that so many Ordinances should not have been issued. I personally think it is not a light matter to be ignored. Certain observations have been made by my predecessor Shri Mavalankar based on very sound judgement. I would invite the attention of the Government to see that there is real emergency or urgency justifying the issue of an Ordinance.

Seeing Government persistently adamant, members raised this matter in House vociferously on November 22, 1971. Speaker, thereupon, gave vent to his exasperation in these words: "All I can say is that I do not approve of an Ordinance just at the time when the House is about to meet." On November 17, 1980, when the Minister of Parliamentary Affairs laid on the Table 10 Ordinances issued under Article 123 of the Constitution, members spoke vehemently against them. The then Speaker Dr. Bal Ram Jakhar observed: "My distinguished predecessors have made observations in regard to these matters from time to time in the past. They did not approve of the issue of Ordinances on the eve of Parliament session. I agree with them."

The then President Dr. Shanker Dayal Sharma on March 19, 1996 observed: "I would like to inform that independent of the relative intrinsic merits of the Ordinances proposed, promulgating these Ordinances would appear to be inappropriate and contrary to the canons of Constitutional propriety in view of circumstances existing at this particular juncture."

The practice of issuing ordinance at the fag end of the prorogation of the session of Parliament is still continuing. On January 12, 2005, the Union Cabinet decided to bring in an ordinance to amend certain sections of the Code of Criminal Procedure. The ordinance would empower the government to withhold the notification of controversial provisions—such as those opposed by lawyers and other social activists, like making bail and anticipatory bail stringent for hardened criminals. The amendment will also help the government implement provisions that are perceived as people friendly. The proposed ordinance would prohibit arrest of women after sunset and before sunrise except in unavoidable circumstances. It will also prohibit the detention of under trials beyond the maximum period of imprisonment for the alleged offence. Significantly, The Code of Criminal Procedure (Amendment) Bill 2005 was passed by both Houses of Parliament and later okayed by the President on June 23, 2005. Now the question arises why the Government could not incorporate these provisions in the amendment Bill when it was being debated in the Parliament? For what reasons the Bill, even after it had received the assent of the President, was not notified throughout such a long period of time. And finally, does it not amount to bypassing the Parliament when ordinance is issued after it had passed the Bill on the same law? The government promulgated nine ordinances in the year 2009 alone. This is the second highest figure for the past decade.

The above is the latest example how ordinance-making power has been used un-abashedly to bypass Parliament. Author is of the opinion that whenever a situation arises wherein it is felt absolutely essential to promulgate an ordinance, then the matter should be referred to a Committee comprising Speaker of Lok Sabha, Chairman of Rajya Sabha and leaders of Opposition in both the houses. While sending the Draft ordinance to President, the views expressed by this Committee should accompany as its Annexure. This will work as check-and-balance to discourage the growing tendency of issuing ordinances.

Cash—for—Query—Scam and MP Lad Scheme—Another Chink in Parliamentary System

In its entire five decade long working, Parliamentary system in India has never faced the magnitude of crisis as it had to face in December 2005. When 11 of its MPs were caught on camera taking bribes for raising questions and seeking share of their Local Area Development Fund, it appeared as if the whole edifice is crumbling. Even the seasoned Parliamentarians had to hang their heads in shame. Conscience and credibility, both saw their lowest ebb. Never before Parliament had to pass a resolution expelling nearly half a dozen of its MPs. Raising a question and answering the same in Parliament is an expensive proposition. Nearly 250 questions are admitted every day in each of the two houses of Parliament. On an average the government answers 75,000 questions every year in Parliament. If such an exercise is subjected to money-spinning by the members themselves, then it is bound to derail the whole system. In that case, vested interests will come to dominate the Parliamentary debates through the MPs sold like commodity.

The historic decision of expulsion of 11 MPs in the wake of scam finds no parallel in the history of any other Parliamentary system. In 1994, in UK, three MPs had received 1000 pounds each for asking a question in Parliament. In Australia, opposition leader was under scanner for receiving $1,10,000 from PWC. He was exonerated of all charges because of a loophole in the law. In U.S. also, Cunningham, a member of House of Representatives was tried for receiving bribes to swing defence deals. Cunnigham had to plead guilty and his membership was suspended.

The revelations made public by the sting operation named as "Operation Duryodhana" was enough to shock the conscience of the nation. The questions for which they took money ranging from Rs. 10,000 to Rs. 1,10,000 pertained to the welfare of Small Scale Industries, SEBI Inquiry into 2004 Stock market crash and such other matters of public interests. According to the statement, several MPs also wanted an annual fee of rupees five to six lakh to put in as many proxy questions as it wanted. Surprisingly, some of the MPs were wary of sting operations. Yet it did not stop them from taking money. Narendra Kushwaha of the BSP even enquired— Hope you are not tapping all this. Don't get me into the trouble. Another MP, Pradeep Gandhi sniffed at the undercover operation and checked the bags before pocketing the cash. In fact the incident of taking money to raise question is not a recent one. It reminds people of the incident when Keshav Dev Malviya, a Minister in Pandit Jawahar Lal Nehru's cabinet demanded Rs. 10,000 from an industrialist for the purpose of election expenses. When Nehru came to know of this, he called Malviya, enquired about the whole matter. He also showed to him a copy of the letter written by him seeking financial assistance. When Malviya could not deny the letter he had written, Nehru immediately asked him to resign from the Cabinet.

In another case, H.G. Mudgal, a member of Provisional Parliament (Prior to the coming into force of the Constitution) received financial and business advantage from the Bombay Bullion Association for canvassing support and making propaganda in Parliament on problems like option business, stamp duty, etc. P.S. Nadkarni, an official of the Bombay Government's Finance Department was a nominee of the Government on the Board of Bullion Association. In a meeting of the Board on March 9, 1951, the President of the Association told the members that H.G. Mudgal, an MP had offered to drum up support for the Association in Parliament for a fee of Rs. 20,000. Mudgal was paid Rs. 10,000 initially of the agreed sum of Rs. 5000. On getting money, Mudgal gave notice for the question on March 20, 1951 and also wrote to Finance Minister C.D. Deshmukh asking him to grant an interview to the President of Bombay Bullion Association. On getting wind of the shady deal, Nehru summoned Mudgal and asked him to explain. When matter was raised in Lok Sabha, Nehru told the House that conduct of Mudgal was highly derogatory and objectionable. He proposed for expelling Mudgal from Parliament. But even before the House could have voted for the Resolution, Mudgal tendered resignation.

The cash-for-query scam which hit the headlines, left the whole political system badly mauled and exposed. It raised many eyebrows. It was the credibility in the Parliamentary system which was at stake. People doubted that the practice of getting cash for putting up questions might have been continuing since long. It is but for the use of advanced high tech system in Sting Operation which has exposed the corruption at such a high level. Several people did not appreciate the method adopted in carrying out sting operation as it had the ingredient of deceitful trapping and against the healthy trends of journalism. This argument was, however, countered by an adage that hard situation demands hard decision just as chronic diseases entails harsh treatment.

Looking to the Constitutional remedies to prevent such ugly incidents to recur, there is hardly any provision which can be cited as prescription to cure the ailment like this. An indepth study of the Constitutional provisions would led us to believe that all the expelled members could not have been expelled as they had not earned any disqualification enumerated in Article 102 of the Constitution. Under Article 102, the power to punish for breach of privilege does not include the power to expel a member from the membership of the House. Arun Jaitley, a Senior Advocate and General Secretary of BJP, in his Article 'Bend rules to lay them down' the *Hindustan Times*, 27-12-2005) raised a constitutional debate as to whether the width of power of Parliament with regard to breach of privilege includes the power to expel. According to him privileges under Article 105 of the Constitution are not codified. The tenure of a member, which is a constitutionally defined tenure, could be cut short for reasons of disqualifications as contained in Article 102 and for reasons of breach of privilege Article 105. He tried to build a case that any decision of Parliament to expel members would only be overstretching of the power which is otherwise not vested in it.

The question whether a Member of Parliament comes within the definition of "Public Servant" for the purpose of Prevention of Corruption Act 1988 came up for decision in *P.V. Narasimha Rao* vs. *State*. The charge framed against Rao was that he and some others entered into a criminal conspiracy to bribe certain accused, namely, Suraj Mandal and other MPs to induce them to vote against the motion of no confidence moved against Rao's government in Lok Sabha. Charge-sheets were filed against both the bribe givers and bribe takers. Special judge, trying the accused persons, held that members of Parliament are holding a public office and accepting illegal gratification for exercising their franchise in a particular manner is a punishable offence under the Prevention of Corruption Act 1988. The High Court agreed with the verdict of Special Judge and confirmed that MPs are public servant within the meaning of Prevention of Corruption Act. On hearing the appeal against this judgment, a five judge constitution Bench of the Supreme Court, too unanimously concluded that a member of Parliament is a 'public servant' and the Prevention of Corruption Act is applicable to them also. The question relating to immunity enjoyable by MPs under Article 105(2) also came up. The judges were, however, not unanimous about the applicability of Constitutional immunity conferred upon MPs under Article 105(2). The point which led them to the dissent was over the question as to how far Article 105(2) can be interpreted so as to extend its sweep to the extent of bribe giving or bribe taking. It could not have been the intention of the framers of the Constitution to bring the offence like bribe-giving or its taking within the ambit of the Constitutional immunity. If that be the case, then it would have the implications of expanding the immunity to include any other criminal offence and all that would be required is to somehow associate the same with the discharge of parliamentary work or duties relating to debates in Parliament.

As the Prevention of Corruption Act does not specify any authority competent to remove a Member of Parliament from membership, it creates a legal vacuum. Moreover, permission of the Speaker in the case of Lok Sabha and Chairman in case of Rajya Sabha is required to be obtained before filing a charge-sheet in respect of criminal offences committed by MPs. It was this legal vaccum followed by Constitutional immunity conferred upon Article 105(2) of the Constitution which led to the acquittal of the

MPs. In no other Parliamentary system, such a lacuna exists. If we look at the position as prevalent in U.K., the offer of money or other advantage to any Member of Parliament for the promoting of any matter whatsoever pending or to be transacted in Parliament is high crime and misdemeanor. In terms of Resolution passed by House of Commons in 1695, it amounts to the 'subversion of the English Constitution'. An attempt to bribe a member of Legislative Assembly is a criminal offence in Australia. There is no immunity insofar as such criminal offence is concerned. Same is the position in Canada where giving or taking of bribe by a legislator constitutes an offence.

While analysing this position, National Commission to Review the working of the Constitution, in its Report Vol. II Book 1 recommended for inserting in Article 105 the following clause to be read as 3(A). It reads as follows:

3(A) (i) Nothing in clause (1), (2) or (3) shall bar the prosecution of a Member of Parliament, in any Court of law, for an offence involving receiving or accepting, whether directly or indirectly, and whether for his own benefit or for the benefit of any other person in whom he is interested, any kind of monetary or other valuable consideration for voting in a particular manner or for not voting, as the case may be, in a House of Parliament.

(ii) No court shall take cognisance of the offence mentioned in sub-clause (i) of this clause, except with the previous sanction of the Committee constituted under sub-clause (iii) of this clause.

(iii) The Committee referred to in sub-clause (ii) shall be a permanent committee constituted by the President. It shall comprise five Members of Parliament drawn from the Lok Sabha and Rajya Sabha (in proportion of 3:2) nominated by the President in consultation with the Speaker of the Lok Sabha and the Chairman of the Rajya Sabha. The terms of the members of the Committee and other incidental matters may be such as may be notified by the President in the order constituting the committee.

10

MP Area Development Scheme—Irregularities Galore

One scheme which finds no parallel in the annals of Parliamentary democracy and has been the subject of so much controversy and odium is the MP Area Development Scheme which was commenced by Narasimha Rao government in December 1993. His government was in minority and was in dire need of introducing several measures to strengthen his position. Under the scheme each MP is provided Rs. 2 crores every year for carrying out development works in his constituency. It was in sharp contrast to the parliamentary system for the simple reason that an amalgamation of executive power with legislative power was sought under this scheme. Before launching the scheme of providing fund to MPs, he chose not to set up any committee or seek any financial advice from Comptroller and Auditor General, Planning Commission or other institute capable to render independent advice. He went ahead and allocated whopping sums to implement the scheme. Ever since then, the scheme has remained under clouds of controversies and charges of irregularities. Under the scheme, funds are released and deposited in nationalized Banks and carry interest at the usual rates. As per guidelines, all funds released are non-lapsable. In other words, funds that remain unutilized in a particular year can be carried forward to the following year. Although, the grants are valid for one year under Article 112 of the Constitution, no such condition is created for funds under MP LAD scheme. An MP can suggest individual works costing not more than Rs. 25 lakhs per work either in his own constituency or even outside. An MP can order for taking up the works like buildings for schools, hostels, libraries and other buildings of educational institutions, construction of tubewells, water tanks for providing water, construction of roads, approach roads, link road, culverts, bridges, common shelters, sports clubs, hospitals, multigyms, forestry, parks, desilting of ponds, gober gas plants, non-conventional energy system, irrigation embankments, creches, reading rooms, crematorium, drains, gutters, footpaths, pathways, bus-sheds, veterinary aid center and computer education projects in High Schools, etc. However, an MP can not undertake the works for constructing commercial buildings, Memorials and places of religious worships.

Finding the infirmities and inherent loopholes in the scheme, a large number of MPs took full advantage and indulged in serious irregularities. Barely five years after the scheme was brought into practice, serious lapses emerged and Comptroller and Auditor General (CAG) came out with revelations highlighting all sorts of irregularities. It referred to instances of diversion of funds for purposes other than admissible. The fund was misused for executing commercial and private projects besides expenditure on religious places. CAG found cases of "irregular award of contracts", "deficient execution of work", "excess expenditure", "irregularities in purchases", "frauds" and "misappropriation". Now the latest in the series, which acted as a blow, came from the sting operation in which MPs were caught on camera while receiving the money as their share under MP LAD scheme.

The then Lok Sabha Speaker Somnath Chatterjee favoured scrapping the scheme as it eats up Rs. 1600 crores each year. The Planning Commission pointed numerous flaws in execution of these funds. While examining the working of this scheme, the National Commission to Review the working of Constitution also recommended for its withdrawal as it found the scheme as inconsistent with the spirit of federalism and encroached on areas under Panchayat Raj institutions. The scheme has often been likened to the benevolent feudal landlord who would dole out favours to please a selected few. It has set precedents for several state governments to withdraw the similar scheme in respect of MLAs. An editorial published in the *Hindustan Times* (December 22, 2005) made an appeal for scrapping the scheme. It stated that MPs have a free hand to dole out contracts that have nothing tangible to show at the end. Part of the money mysteriously ends up in the pockets of the very MPs whose job it is to spend it on developmental work. According to rough figure, at least Rs. 7,500 crores are doled out to MPs during their five year terms. Most of this is not used and a substantial part of the rest is used for developing some very individual wallets. Another aspect relates to the lack of monitoring and absence of proper auditing of the account of expenditure under the scheme. Knowing that expenditure incurred under the scheme is not open for any fair audit, MPs consider the fund as their dole and feel free to indulge in irregularities. In no other country, such a scheme is provided without laying down any mechanism for control and supervision.

In spite of the serious irregularities pointed out by CAG in its report, government led by Congress decided to continue the scheme. Successive governments too could not get rid of it because of pressures which were entailed by any coalition governments. Far from scrapping the scheme, several Congress leaders including Priya Ranjan Dasmunshi demanded for enhancement of the annual grant from Rs. 2 crores to Rs. 5 crores per annum. Nobody has explained why MP LAD scheme should not be covered under Right to Information Act. Why the people who elect their representative should be deprived of their right to know what their MP has done out of the funds made available to him out of taxes paid by them? Demands for withdrawing the scheme were echoed at all levels and entire national media had spoken against it.

MP LAD scheme has embroiled in several controversies involving seven MPs caught on camera in a sting operation by a TV channel. A TV channel in a sting operation called "Operation Chakravyuh" showed to the country how MPs were seen asking for kickbacks under the scheme a kitty of

Rs. 8,000 crore—to be spent at the discretion of members of both houses. The sting, which came when House committees are examining the cash-for-query scam, also featured lackluster names with the exception of the flamboyant and controversial former Goa CM and south Goa MP Churchil Alemao (Congress). BJP once again had a higher head count of MPs—Faggan Singh Kulaste, Sidhi MP Chandra Pratap Singh who has already been tainted in "Operation Duryodhan" and Ramswaroop Koli from Bayana in Rajasthan. The then Lok Sabha Speaker Somnath Chatterjee who had launched a strong campaign to settle down the discretion of MPs in implementation of MPLADS, said he was ashamed. An ex-MP Era Sezhiyan in his book *MPLADs Concept, Confusion and Contradictions* joined the tirade against the scheme by calling it as "assault on the Constitution" and demanded it to be scrapped.

Hardly the dust raised by "Operation Chakravyuha" could have settled when the controversy over Navin Chawla, the then Election Commissioner (Now CEC) came to surface with bitterest ever criticism from all political parties except Congress. Vociferous demands were raised for removing Chawla from his post.

Controversy over doling out of funds to the tune of about Rs. 85 lacs from MPLADS by Congress MPs A.A. Khan, R.P. Goenka, Ambika Soni, Dr. Karan Singh and A.R. Kidwai to a Jaipur based Lala Chaman Lal Education Trust arose when *Times Now* TV Channel claimed that the trusts were being run under patronage of Navin Chawla, then Election Commissioner. The trust was also allotted six acres of land by the Congress government in Rajasthan when Ashok Gehlot was the Chief Minister. The land was allotted at one-tenth of market price. While the Trust was stated to had been run by someone else, he was using his own letterhead as Principal Secretary to Pondicherry Government seeking financial assistance. Chawla, however, denied having received any money not even from MPLAD or even from any person after his appointment as Election Commissioner. "Previous to that I could not dream that I was going to be appointed EC."

K.K. Venugopal, a Senior Lawyer and Constitutional Expert argued in Supreme Court that MPLAD scheme is invalid and unconstitutional. Appearing for Bhim Singh, leader of the Panthers party, Mr. Venugopal said powers to MPs to implement projects meant that executive powers had been taken over by the legislature. But Chawla refused to resign and later promoted to the post of Chief Election Commissioner in spite of all vociferous protests from every political quarter.

Congress has a history of subverting constitutional organs for its political advantages. Often controversies arose over appointments to the constitutional offices in Election Commission, Courts or Governors in States, etc. being motivated by political consideration and raised controversies. In 1973 when A.N. Ray was appointed Chief Justice of Supreme Court after superseding seniors like K.S. Hegde, Grover and Shelat, a national debate rocked as this was taken as a move towards undermining the Constitutional institutions. Controversy arose when in an un-precedented move, M.S. Gill, Ex-Chief Election Commissioner was appointed Ministry for Sports. Similar controversy arose when Kiran Bedi was ignored while appointing Police Commissioner in Delhi despite being senior.

MPLAD Scheme as commenced in India has no parallel in any democratic system of any country. It is unique for the reason that it is not ordinarily open for any indepth investigation. Nobody can invoke Right to Information and no official can question the feasibility of work or project sanctioned under this scheme. Comptroller and Auditor General of India has already raised serious observations against the scheme and its implementation. The scheme came under judicial scrutiny with the Supreme Court referring a bunch of petitions challenging its validity to a Constitution Bench. A bench comprising Chief Justice Y.K. Sabharwal and Justices C.K. Thakker and P.K. Balasubramanyam observed that the petitions raised some important questions of law that needed to be settled. The petitioners—Jammu and Kashmir National Panthers Party and Lok Sevak Sangh, an NGO had sought scrapping of the scheme, claiming about Rs 5,000 crore of public money is being misused by elected representatives. They had argued that the scheme was violative of Article 14 of the Constitution (Right to Equality) as it gave arbitrary powers to an MP without checks and balances. MPs are not complying with the guidelines issued for the implementation of the scheme. There is no participation of people or local area councilors, panchayat leaders as the entire sum under the scheme is placed at the discretion of an MP. Though all and one including the then Lok Sabha Speaker Somnath Chatterjee have spoken against the continuation of this scheme, not much could be done to scrap it.

Though opposition parties have criticized the functioning of the scheme, their protest is not as vociferous as it should have been. Since the scheme has become a part of our legislative functioning, almost all the States have followed suit by adopting the similar schemes for their MLAs. Thus not only in Centre but also at States level, the scheme has come to stay as part of the political system. Once this system firms up its roots in entire federal system with the support of all political parties, it would be well nigh impossible to scrap it unless there is revolutionary change or some drastic order passed by the apex court of the country. It is in fact a sort of bribe under official recognition to dole out to legislators for continuing the arrangement in which a party has cobbled up a majority to form government. No sting operation recording MPs taking bribe or kickback is going to help the process against scheme.

11

Substantial Decrease in Periods of Sessions—Bureaucracy Taking Parliament for Granted

A persistent decrease in number of sittings of Parliament is another factor attributable to the decline of Parliament. At the present juncture when the country is taking strides in every field, complexities in legislations are becoming evident into new fields, budget allocations are showing tremendous increase, the work of Parliament should also keep pace with the increasing workload. On the contrary Bills are being passed without fruitful discussion. Twice in the history when budgets were passed in five minutes without any debate whatsoever. Describing the present state of affairs, Som Nath Chatterjee, the then Lok Sabha Speaker, himself remarked Parliament is becoming a "laughing stock for the people of the country". Bureaucracy is just taking Parliament for granted. Due to limited sittings, Parliament finds little time to exercise control over administration in an effective manner.

A Table showing fall in number of sittings beginning from 1st Lok Sabha to 13th is added below:

Lok Sabha	Time Spent (Hrs)	No. of sitting days
1st 1952-57	3784	677
2nd 1957-62	3652	567
3rd 1962-67	3733	578
4th 1967-70	3029	469
5th 1971-77	4071	613

6th 1977-79	1753	267
7th 1980-84	3324	464
8th 1985-89	3224	485
9th 1989-91	754	109
10th 1991-96	2528	423
11th 1996-97	814	125
12th 1998-99	575	88
13th 1999-2004	919	356
14th 2004-09	992	332

Mackintosh, a Political Scientist has observed—"All over the world, where democratic systems of Government survives, it is being said that legislatures are losing ground to the bureaucracy. The reason is complexity of law, procedure and paucity of time." Under such phenomenon firming up roots, Parliament can not be expected to do justice to its assigned role. Its lots of time is wasted in interruptions, raising point of orders, adjournments and other disorderly scenes. A study reveals how much of precious times was wasted in disorderly scenes. The following table reflects this growing trends:

Lok Sabha	Time on disorderly Scenes (Hours)
10th 1991-96	279
11th 1996-97	45
12th 1998-99	68
13th 1999-2004	258
14th 2004-09	423

While the Government does not want a longer duration of the session, MPs too are wary of it for the reason that they have pre-occupation in their constituencies and other works relating to various committees and political meetings and conferences. Due to their constituencies getting first preference, they find hardly any time to thoroughly study the different Bills before Parliament. The lack of time followed by lack of interest does not permit them to remain present in the House and take active participation in debate.

If this remains a trend in times to come, then further erosion in the powers and performances of the Parliament can not be ruled out. In spite of all talks of supremacy, it is fast losing its dominating position in the political set up for reasons more practical than constitutional.

The decline of Parliament became more pronounced in the 14th Lok Sabha which would earn the epitaph of the darkest chapter in India's high temple of democracy. It acquired several firsts. The Prime Minister was not the leader of the House. Five tainted Ministers adorned the Treasury Benches, shrugged off as "compulsions of coalition politics". The Speaker was expelled by his own party. Innumerable scams rocked each session every year. Leading to another unprecedented situation when the Left parties moved a privilege motion against the Prime Minister in the Lok Sabha for his failure to report to the House before operationalising the Indo-US Nuclear deal as promised by him. The Speaker rejected the motion by stating that the privilege issue could be raised only in Rajya Sabha as the Prime Minister was a member there. Since Congress was in majority in Rajya Sabha, it was considered meaningless to move a motion in that house. In the last session of 14th Lok Sabha as many as 18 important bills were passed in a short span of 15 minutes without any debate. Surprisingly, on the last day of 14th Lok Sabha, 34 bills lapsed while the fate of 46 remained in limbo. Most worrisome aspect was the marked decrease in the number of days on which the two houses met. The House hit on all time low when the Lok Sabha functioned only for 32 days. Notwithstanding the political consensus that Parliament should meet for a minimum of 100 days in a year, it met only for 66 days in 2007, 32 days in 2008 and 64 days in 2009. In 2008 when the Monsoon session was adjourned to December, Parliamentary Minister was criticized for scuttling the Parliament. His cryptic remark was "Say anything you like." Such a remark was unpalatable and against all cannons of parliamentary conventions.

Substantial decrease in number of sessions had been a subject of controversy for the last 40 years. Attempts to bypass Parliament reflected not merely in issuing ordinance during the session or not informing the Parliament about several important deals or treaties but also in reducing the sessions considerably. In the most diabolical and dangerous dimension of making the Lok Sabha insignificant, its sessions were curtailed repeatedly during the last four decades. The controversy began in 1975 when several MPs had to write a letter to the Speaker of Lok Sabha inviting his attention to the denigration of Parliament and erosion in the well-established conventions and precedents which are so essential for its working.

From Members of Parliament to the Speaker of the Lok Sabha

21 June 1975

To

The Hon'ble Speaker
Lok Sabha
NEW DELHI

Sir,

We are perturbed that summons for the Monsoon Session of Parliament this year have not been received so far. It has been the practice in the past to have the Monsoon Session from the middle of July and to send the summons by the first week of June. It is pertinent to invite your kind attention to a decision taken by the General Purposes Committee of Lok Sabha at their sitting held on April 22, 1955 and their following recommendation on the time-table of the three sessions of the Lok Sabha to be held every year:

(1)	(2)	(3)
Session	*Date of commencement*	*Date of termination*
Budget Session	February 1	May 7
Monsoon Session	July 15	Sep 15
Winter Session	November 5 or Four days after Deepavali whichever Is later.	December 22

The Cabinet also agreed with these recommendations and as far as possible the sessions are held round about these dates every year.

We are afraid that this time-honoured practice accepted by the Cabinet and implemented hitherto appears to be in danger of being given a go-by.

We are aware that as the constitutional head, the President has to summon the Houses of Parliament to meet. It is also clear that the Constitution only stipulates that a period of six months will not elapse between the concluding day of one session and the first day of the next. But parliamentary democracy functions and flourishes not only or the letter of the Constitution but also on the practices and the conventions evolved. Although the Constitution only lays down that at least two sessions will be held in a year it was the practice to hold three sessions. When there was a lame-duck session after the elections, we had one more session. This practice, we are afraid, is sought to be given up to meet the convenience of the Prime Minister. There has been a demand, rightly so, that the House should meet earlier than usual to discuss the implications of the judgement given by the Allahabad High Court. Instead of advancing the usual date, there has been a deliberate delay. The tendency to dishonour the practice will, it is apprehended, embolden the executive to override the conventions and subvert the Constitution itself. The appeal preferred by the Prime Minister to the Supreme Court does not affect the issues of morality and propriety raised by the judgement of the High Court. The decision of the Supreme Court in the stay petition is not relevant to these issues. It is inconceivable by any standard of parliamentary democracy that a person who has been held guilty of corrupt practices should continue as Prime Minister. She has every right to appeal to the highest court of the land and obtain its decision. But till the proved charges have not been set aside and she is not absolved of all corrupt practices as proved in the High Court, propriety, rectitude and convention require that she steps down from her office immediately.

As custodian of the rights and privileges of the House and as one who is specially responsible for the proper working of the parliamentary democracy in this country, you, more than anybody else, must be concerned. At this time of crisis, when democratic conventions are being flouted and parliamentary traditions scuttled, and autocracy is being enthroned in the place of democracy with the strange plea that a particular individual is indispensable to our country, we look to you to uphold the traditions of democracy. We are not here to suggest who should be the leader of the party which enjoys a majority in the House. It is the internal affair of that party. But we are of the firm opinion that with such a judgement from a High Court, Mrs. Indira Gandhi has lost the moral authority to continue in the office of the Prime Minister. If she wins her appeal in the Supreme Court and if her party so desires she may return to power later. The said order does not absolve nor does it negative the judgement of the High Court. We do not want that the Prime Minister should oblige the opposition, but we feel that she should fulfil her obligations towards parliamentary democracy.

We, therefore, request you to impress upon the President and Mrs. Indira Gandhi the need to observe the well-established conventions and practices of democracy.

Yours sincerely,

S.N. Mishra
Era Sezhiyan
Jagannathrao Joshi
Madhu Limaye
V.R. Scindia
Jyotirmoy Basu
Samar Guha
Erasmo de Sequeira

POOR QUALITY OF DEBATES AND PANDEMONIUMS

In its report "Governance and Development-2006", National Social Watch revealed that 14th Lok Sabha wasted 26 per cent of its time on pandemonium and stalling of proceedings. It is the highest in comparison to 11th Lok Sabha wasting 5.28%, 12th wasting 10.66%, 13th with 24.40%. According to data published, Parliament is fast turning into a slogan-shouting stage than a debating forum. It is paradoxical that MPs find no time to participate in any constructive debates. A large number of Bills are passed without proper discussion. There have been instances when Bills involving far reaching implications were passed without debate. When it comes to settle political scores, they join chorus to sit for hours together and prove their debating skills. On number of occasions, Parliament sessions were boycotted for several days. In most cases, slogan shouting MPs came to the well of the House and forestalled the session. In July/August 1994, opposition did not let the Parliament to work for about 16 days. No business could be transacted and loss on public exchequer was incalculable. In 1996 when telecom scandal involving Sukhram came to light, Parliament could not transact any business and remained under adjournments for 13 days. Over 10.5 per cent of the time of 10th Lok Sabha was wasted in such hold ups. In 2000, Parliament was not allowed to work for eight days on the issue of Gujarat Government permitting its employees to become members of Rashtriya Swayam Sewak Sangh. The matter, though pertained to the state of Gujarat, yet the opposition led by Congress forestalled the working of Parliament for such a long period of time.

From 1992 onwards, it has become a ritual for the MPs to rake up Ayodhya's Babri Mosque and seek adjournment. In fact the ritual of chest beating on every 6th December emanates from the politics of placating minorities and garnering their votes. Lok Sabha had since then faced adjournments for 111 hours on this issue. Adding to the series came Gujarat riots in February 2002 when in the run up to Godhra killings, communal riots spread all over Gujarat. Parliament was adjourned for 150 hours only on this issue.

Bofors had also its share to stall proceedings for more than 250 hours. Its ghost is still haunting the country. In January 2006, it fell heavily upon the Law Minister when Supreme Court directed the Union Government and the CBI to take steps to ensure that status quo was maintained vis-a-vis the two London Bank accounts of Italian businessman Ottavio Quattrochchi, an accused in Bofors case. Hearing a petition seeking the Court's intervention to stop the transfer of Rs. 26 crore lying in Quattrochhi's accounts in public interest, the Supreme Court sought clarification from the Government as to whether the decision to defreeze the accounts was taken pursuant to any action on the part of CBI or Centre. Did the Government want defreezing of the account was the straight question which the Government could not reply. This shows how for even such matters, Parliament has been ineffective to reign the Government and ultimately it was the Court's directives which led the whole matter to stage of investigation.

In 2004 when 14th Lok Sabha was constituted, forestalling of Parliament session scaled new heights. On the issue of tainted Ministers, opposition forced Speaker to adjourn the House repeatedly. On the issues arising out of Governors' politically motivated actions in Goa, Jharkhand and Bihar, Parliament witnessed uprorious scenes, slogan shouting and persistent bedlam. Nanavati Commission's report on 1984 Delhi riots came as another reason for the opposition to raise furore in the house. Lok Sabha, again had to be adjourned. Som Nath Chatterjee, Speaker was seen losing cool while trying to restore order in the House. At one point of time he expressed his deep anguish and offered to resign from the office of Speaker of Lok Sabha. UN's Volcker's report and its indictment of Congress Party and the then External Minister Natwar Singh having received the money in Food-for-Oil scam saw the Parliament in a state of pandemonium yet again. BJP the main opposition party demanded the resignation of Natwar Singh. To prevent an embarrassing position, his portfolio of External Affairs ministry was withdrawn and his status was confined to the Cabinet Minister without portfolio. Subsequently, he had to tender resignation from the Cabinet when India's ambassador to Croatia, Aniel Matherani, in his interview to *India Today* made revelations on the dealings involving the Minister and his son. Opposition did not let the Parliament to work for five days. Speaker had to adjourn the House repeatedly. These frequent adjournments of the House proceedings create sensations and drew strong public sentiments. Knowing this opposition used this as technique to built up public opinion and then extract resignation from the delinquent Ministers. This technique has paid off well. Opposition has been able to extract resignation from Shibu Soren, Jayaprakash Yadav, Jagdish Tytler, Sajjan Kumar and Natwar Singh.

Apart from shouting slogans, raising din and disorderly scenes, MPs have indulged in acts of indiscipline and disrespect to the chair. At one occasion, a senior MP and former Railway Minister Mamta Bannerjee hurled papers at Deputy Speaker Charanjit Atwal when he was presiding over the Lok Sabha. The provocation arose out of rejection of her adjournment motion on "illegal infiltration of Bangladeshi". Her motion was accompanied by a 'fake voters list' which contained numerous names of Bangladeshi nationals. Her act of showing disrespect to the Chair and hurling papers on his person was assailed by MPs from all political parties. She followed up her angry outburst by tendering resignation from the House. The letter that she had scribbled was later turned down by the Speaker on the ground that "it was not proper letter of resignation". Terming the House as the highest forum in the country, the Speaker said it was becoming a laughing stock for the people of the country.

As the winnability and not the merit is criteria for political parties to select candidates for election, the quality of debates and ability to utilise parliamentary techniques are bound to suffer. What to talk of speaking extempore on burning issues or raising adjournment motions, most of the MPs are yet to excel in picking up issues and raise probing questions. For Question Hour, which is the first business for Lok Sabha to transact, thousands of questions are received by the Lok Sabha Secretariat. But less than 40 per cent of them were accepted.

The reasons for rejecting such a big number of questions were varied and include lack of relevancy, poor framing of question and frivolity of the matter, etc. The following table would reveal how less than 40 per cent questions are usually admitted for reply:

Parliament Questions Admitted for Reply

Lok Sabha	Total Notices for Questions	Admitted	Percentage
First (1952-57)	71,907	43,350	60
Second (1957-62)	1,33,328	62,800	47
Third (1962-67)	1,62,334	58,440	36
Fourth (1967-70)	2,64,742	93,538	35
Fifth (1971-77)	2,52,700	98,606	39
Sixth (1977-79)	1,37,045	51,209	37
Seventh (1980-84)	2,69,221	1,02,697	38
Eighth (1985-89)	2,50,098	98,390	39
Ninth (1989-91)	75,228	21,550	29
Tenth (1991-96)	3,30,325	90,605	27
Eleventh (1996-97)	96,863	23,681	24
Twelfth (1998-99)	72,934	15,579	21
Thirteenth (1999-2004)	1,52,208	37,994	25

A glance of above table reveals that during thirteenth Lok Sabha 75 per cent of the total questions raised were not admitted. Rejection of such an enormous number of question either reflects that these were either not framed as per the yardsticks or the contents were not found admissible due to their lack of relevance.

Speaking in the Constituent Assembly on the parliamentary system, Dr. Rajendra Prasad had expressed surprise over not providing any qualification for the law-makers. While striking a parallel line between law making and law-enforcing authorities, he questioned the wisdom of not providing any qualifications for law-maker whereas the authorities who are supposed to implement law have to fulfill academic qualifications besides undergoing rigorous training programmes before assuming the charge. As the country was in the grip of severe illiteracy with nearly 70 per cent of population illiterate and also as majority of political leaders were not even graduate, any act of providing qualifications would have deprived them of contesting elections. But this is not the position now as the country has acquired higher literacy.

Absenteeism during proceedings of House is becoming marked feature of Parliamentary system. Even during Question Hour which is described as "essence of Parliamentary Democracy" has come under the spell of sharp absenteeism. An unprecedented scene emerged during first winter session of 15th Lok Sabha when 34 MPs were found missing after submitting questions. For the first time ever, Question Hour fell through as MP after MP cutting across party lines, who had listed their names for questions were found to be absent. Parliamentary experts were astonished and could not recollect such an incident that had ever happened in the Parliamentary proceedings. To most it seemed another shameful pointer to the lack of seriousness with which our MPs take their job. Speaker Meira Kumar had to adjourn the House in exasperation. The collapse of Question Hour in Lok Sabha due to absent MPs sent shock wages in entire political circle and UPA Chairperson Sonia Gandhi had to intervene personally calling for introducing some effective mechanism to curb this tendency. It was suggested in several quarters that an MP who is found absent after his question admitted must be debarred from submitting questions for a certain period as deterrent measure. Perhaps MPs did not realize that it was the Question Hour query that blew the lid off the first ever major scam over Mundhra which led to the resignation of the then Finance Minister T.T. Krishnamachari. Sometimes MPs do not know what questions are being asked in their names. They do not come prepared to raise supplementary questions and lack zeal and enthusiasm to expose chinks in the bureaucratic set up which is one of the purposes behind question hour. According to Constitutional expert Shri Subhash Kashyap, Speaker can ask the listed question even if a questioner is absent. But the provision is rarely used.

It is not just Question Hour where MPs play truant. Attendance of Parliamentary standing committees that vet the functioning of ministries is another indicator of how serious our MPs are about their work. According to details published in the *Times of India*, an audit for 2007-08 of the functioning of standing committees during the last Lok Sabha reveals shocking details, with many MPs earning the dubious distinction of not having attended a single meeting in the entire year. Screen queen-turned-MP Jaya Prada, who triggered a virtual war in Samajwadi Party over her renomination from Rampur, did not show up for any of 26 meetings of the Standing Committee on Information Technology. In contrast, CPM-discard Abdullakutty and Sanjay Shamrao Dhotre attended 23 meetings each, a feat of sorts by current parliamentary standards. Poor attendance by MPs was noticed in the records of all the 12 major committees which met regularly between August 2007 and 2008 to oversee the working of union ministries. This is in spite of the fact that there always remain a scramble among MPs to be on important standing panels since a seat in them gives them leverage with officials. The meetings are hardly an austere affair, with the ministries and public sector undertakings required to foot the bill for tours of members who are invariably lodged in luxurious places and have fleets of cars at their disposal. A report further says that even these incentives are not enough for a few. For instance one MP Janardhan Waghmare skipped all 13 meetings of the agriculture committee, as did former Union Minister Arun Shourie who was a member of defence panel. Likewise, RLD's Anuradha Chaudhary and Nandkumar Chauhan did not show up at any of the 14 meetings of the committee on energy during the year. BSP's Kailash Nath Singh Yadav was marginally better, having attending one meeting. It is not clear what is the difficulty in not laying down the rule to withdraw membership of the committee from such members who remain absent without any substantial reason in such repetitive manner. Why the Parliament can not make it a rule to co-opt other willing member in place of such defaulting members. Perhaps no serious thought is being given to it. With such a scenario continuing, Parliament has already lost its control over the ministries.

12

Criminalisation of Politics—Bane Afflicting Democracy

Politics has often been described as last refuge of the scoundrels. It has received harsher comments from Ronald Reagan, former President of United States who once remarked—"Politics is the second oldest profession. But I have come to realize that it bears resemblance with the first." A famous Persian proverb also says—"A ruler who takes a pinch of salt without paying its price, his officers loot the country." In fact political corruption has ever been regarded as biggest bane and democratic system is unable to root it out. If the rule of survival of the fittest prevails, it is power which makes one fittest. Power corrupts and absolute power corrupts absolutely. It is indeed a sad commentary on our parliamentary system which is not immune from its pitfalls.

In India there has been the substantial increase in number of MPs having criminal records. In the 15th Lok Sabha there are 150 newly elected MPs who have criminal cases pending against them as compared to 128 MPs in 2004 said the study released by National Election Watch. Two MPs—Money Power and Muscle Power can make any person real MP. Under the prevailing system, no person who does not have either of the two or sometimes even both can think of taking risk to enter into electoral battle. The General Election for 15th Lok Sabha witnessed the unabashed display of money power. The number of "Crorepatis" in the 15th Lok Sabha got nearly doubled as compared to 14th Lok Sabha. There are 300 crorepati MPs in new Lok Sabha as compared to 154 in 14th Lok Sabha. What an MP would do after getting elected and what priorities he would pursue is not difficult for anyone to guess. The 14th Lok Sabha which was constituted on 17th May, 2004 with full strength of 545 members was witness to a record number of disqualification including expulsion of 10 MPs for involvement in Cash-for-Query scam and 7 for kickbacks in MP LAD scheme. On the last day of its session, it has the effective strength of only 505 members. This shows that the un-ending scramble for amassing money through fraudulent methods continued unabated for certain section of politicians. Criminalisation of politics is a two-way traffic. While politicians need criminals to meet their political ends, criminals need politicians for getting patronage. A reference to a candidate having record of 174 criminal cases pending against him in Bihar Assembly election shocked the national conscience and our entire polity came in for sharp criticism from all quarters.

Nothing can bring glory to an inglorious deed as politics can bring. The enormity of this feature has belied all talks of probity and accountability in political life. About 700 legislators and 25 MPs have been found with criminal records. In 1998 General Elections, nearly 1500 contestants were found to be involved in criminal offences. This figure showed upward trend in succeeding General Elections, when as many as 3182 contestants were found having criminal records. Nearly 518 candidates were facing trials in criminal cases. A Most Wanted criminal not only in Bihar but also in Delhi and Uttar Pradesh was found contesting election from Bihar Assembly in 2000. A sitting MLA was found contesting while in Jail. Our electoral system became a laughing stock when hardened criminals like bandit Phoolan was able to reach to the portals of Parliament House. The argument that mere filing of charge sheet does not make a person guilty in the eyes of law until he is convicted of an offence is often used as facade to justify continuation in office.

Finding loopholes in electoral laws and pliant administrative set up, criminals began to enter into politics.

Political parties, knowing their clouts and influence, welcomed them with long arms. CBI in its report to Vohra Committee admitted, "all over India, crime syndicates have become a law unto themselves". It reported that "even in the smaller towns and rural areas, muscle-men have become the order of the day. Hired assassins have become part of these organization. The nexus between criminal gangs, police, bureaucracy and politicians has come out clearly in various parts of the country."

In June 2006 Union Home Minister of State Shriprakash Jaiswal declared that to curb such activities a national debate would be welcomed to introduce such constitutional reforms as necessary to restore the faith of people in Parliamentary democracy of the country. He also informed about formation of six member team comprising well-known bureaucrats, Supreme Court Judge and social activists to suggest reforms in the system. He also pleaded that to win an election, a candidate must secure at least 50 per cent votes and not lesser than this. However, nothing concrete happens thereafter and even the suggestions of the team were not made public leaving aside national debate thereon.

The existing criminal justice system which was essentially designed to deal with the individual offences/crimes, is unable to deal with the activities of the insurmountable legal difficulties in attaching/confiscation of the property acquired through virtually running a parallel government pushing the State apparatus into irrelevance.

In 1997, the Election Commission issued an order that candidates for election to State Assemblies and Parliament need to submit an affidavit about their convictions in cases covered by Section 8 of the Representation of the People Act 1951. The EC held that even if the trial court had convicted the candidate, this was enough to attract disqualification. But there are other issues. The Election Commission wrote a letter to the Prime Minister in September 1997 that there were grave incongruities in the existing provisions of sub-sections (1), (2) and (3) of the said Section 8 of the Representation of the People Act 1951, illustrating the case of a rapist, convicted and sentenced to ten years imprisonment, being disqualified only for six years under sub-section (1) and being free to contest elections, even while in prison serving the last four years of his sentence. The commission had suggested that the law may be simplified by amending said Section 8 to provide that whoever is convicted of any offence by a Court of law and sentenced to imprisonment for six months or more should be debarred from contesting elections, for a period totaling the sentence imposed plus an additional six years. This suggestion has been supported by several other organizations and concerned citizens and therefore merits full consideration. Presently, a member of any House is convicted, there is no action for three months and if the case goes for an appeal within this time, then no action is taken till the appeal is disposed off. This may not be very justified. If an elected representative gets convicted on charges related to specific crimes, he should be required to withdraw until he is cleared. It is also worth considering that when political parties are seen to abet criminalization by fielding criminals, there should be some provisions to enable action against them including their derecognition.

In June 2002, Election Commission issued directive to the candidates seeking details of their assets and criminal antecedents. Following these directives, an all party meeting was convened on 8th July 2002 which was attended by leaders of 21 political parties. A unanimous decision was taken to reject the Election Commission directive of June 2002. Taking leaf from the all party meeting, the Government introduced certain amendments in Representation of People Act. A clause 33(B) was inserted by the Representation of the People (Third Amendment) Act 2002. The clause reads as follows:

33(B) Notwithstanding anything contained in any judgment, decrees or order of any court or any direction, order or any other instructions issued by the Election Commission, no candidate shall be liable to disclose or furnish any such information in respect of his election, which is not required to be disclosed or furnished under this Act or the Rules made thereunder.

The government move to debar criminals from contesting election and to arm voters with right to information about candidates was welcomed by political thinkers and media all over the country. However, the constitutional validity of Section 33(B) was challenged before Supreme Court as it was clearly a move to nullify the EC's directive. While hearing the case in the *Union of India* vs. *Association of Democratic Reforms AIR 2002 SC 2112*, Supreme Court observed that the right to get information in a democracy is recognized all over the world and it is a natural right flowing from the concept of democracy. It held that a voter has a fundamental right under Article 19(1)(a) of the Constitution to know the antecedents of a candidate. Such an inalienable right can not be encroached upon by any law, let alone the amendment brought out by inserting Section 33(B) in Representative of Peoples Act. The attempt of the Court was to expand the reach and ambit of the fundamental rights by the process of judicial interpretation. When the right to secure information about a contesting candidate is recognized as an integral part of fundamental right, it follows that its ambit, amplitude and parameters can not be chained and circumscribed for all time to come by an Act. It is not open to the Parliament to stop all further disclosures concerning the candidates in future.

The events took place during the period from October 2005 to January 2006 shook the coalition government at the Centre. Its ministers Jagdish Tytler had to resign in the wake of indictments in Nanavati Commission's report for his involvement in 1984 anti-Sikh riots. Then came UN's Paul Volcker's Report giving names of Natwar Singh, External Affairs Ministers and Congress Party as beneficiaries for kickbacks in Iraq's Food-For-Oil programmes conducted under the aegis of UNO during the regime of Saddam Hussain. Then came Cash-For-Query scam named 'Operation Duryodhana' in which 11 MPs were caught in a sting operation taking bribes for raising questions. In an another sting named 'Operation Chakravyuh' MPs were shown on TV asking for cuts ranging from 5% to 45% for sanctioning funds for constituency development. At a time when a House Committee was inquiring the Cash-For-Query scam, the unfolding of yet another scam involving MPs came as blue from the bolt. It featured names like controversial former Goa Chief Minister and South Goa MP Churchill Alemao of Congress. The news showing Sakshi Maharaj of Samajvadi Party and C.P. Singh of BJP came as shocking and outrageous. Then came the news of confirming the genuineness of taped conversion figuring Ajit Jogi, the then CM of Chhattisgarh offering gratification to MLAs to defect from BJP so as to split the party. Ajit Jogi, being MP (Lok Sabha) was pushed to the wall by this confirmation as analogy on the basis of which 11 MPs were expelled from membership of the House became fully applicable to him also.

Adding to the above melodrama, came the news of Raja Bhaiya (Raghuraj Pratap Singh) joining the UP Cabinet as Minister in Mulayam's team of 60 ministers, the upper limit under the new norms. He was on November 11, 2005 forced to resign from the UP Cabinet when the Supreme Court hearing his bail petition in the Pota case slapped by former Chief Minister Mayawati, rejected his application. He was then taken into judicial custody and shifted to Jabalpur jail. His case is now being heard by Jabalpur court, which granted him bail. Singh's dramatic re-entry within a short span raised many eyebrows. A cornered Mulayam, faced with the growing political strength of Bahujan Samaj Party, tried in desperate to consolidate his base among Thakurs. The fact that Raj Nath Singh, a Thakur was elevated to the post of Party President by BJP also made it imperative for Mulayam Singh to keep Thakurs vote Bank intact in his favour. Taking him into Cabinet provides a latest glaring example of criminalization of politics. It requires amendments in Indian Penal Code, Criminal Procedure Code and Representation of Peoples Act 1951 to make elaborate provisions so as to discourage criminals from entering into politics and cleanse public life. Criminal Justice System also requires to be reviewed. A period of more than three years have elapsed when Malimath Committee gave its report on criminal justice system. In spite of repeated demands from several quarters, the report is yet to be considered for implementation.

13

Governor's Role in Working of Federal System

Once Jawaharlal Nehru was asked as to what were the functions of the Governors. He replied—"to entertain people and make them feel pleased". When Governors complained about Chief Ministers ignoring them persistently, he remarked—"No business to complain". Speaking in the Constituent Assembly, he said "The Governor is a rubber stamp a mere figurehead having absolutely no power worth the name." Dr. Ambedkar, Chairman of the Drafting Committee of the Constitution, expressed opinion that Governor had no functions what to talk of powers; he had only "duties". And the "duties", according to him were mainly two: (1) to retain the Ministry in office and to see when to exercise his pleasure for that purpose in the best possible manner, and (2) to advise the Ministry to warn the Ministry and to suggest to the Ministry alternative and ask for reconsideration. The Governor, he said, was bound to act according to the advice of Ministry. The Governor, like the President, is in reserve gear who comes in when there is an abuse or breakdown of constitutional machinery.

The time, however, proved them otherwise and the perception drawn about the gubernatorial office came to a naught. No other constitutional office has gathered so much bitter controversies as that of Governor. It has been regarded as affront to the working of democracy and obstacle to the smooth working federal system. The voice against the partisan roles of Governors has been so vehement that it had created compulsive situations for the Press, Parliament and Supreme Court to intervene on a number of occasions. It had virtually led to the demand for abolishing the post of Governor. Such a demand can be traced to the views expressed by Mrs. Vijay Lakshmi Pandit, who after resigning as Governor of Maharashtra, openly described the office of Governor as entirely useless and called for its abolition. In 1974, Tamil Nadu Legislative Assembly even passed a Resolution demanding abolition of the post of Governor. The incidents took place in 1982 in Haryana when Bhajan Lal was sworn in as Chief Minister and in 1984 in Andhra Pradesh when N.T. Rama Rao was dismissed from the post of Chief Ministers in spite of having majority were some of the several instances reflecting the misuse of the office of Governor for political purpose. Overnight dismissal of Kalyan Singh Ministry in 1998 and installation of new regime under Jagadambika Pal provides another instance of misuse of office of Governor so much so that Allahabad High Court had to intervene in the whole controversy.

The role played by Governors in Goa, Jharkhand and Bihar in 2004 and 2005 rocked the Parliament and the country. It virtually exposed the hollowness of the whole system marked by gross and blatant misuse of Constitutional provision for furthering political ends. Never before Supreme Court had to issue orders like advancing the date of trial of strength or videography of the proceedings of the house as in the case of Jharkhand. Things reached to such a nadir that even Supreme Court's orders were violated with impunity when the trial of strength was postponed to 15th March 2005.

The office of Governor has been the subject of controversy for not one but several reasons. Firstly, it relates to appointment of Governor. This issue was hotly debated just a few months ago when the UPA Government removed the Governors appointed during NDA Government on the ground of "ideological differences". UPA Government argued that Governors of State must necessarily toe the ideological leanings of the Government at the Centre. This by itself is a very partisan approach because Constitution does not make it an essential criteria that a Governor must toe the ideology of the political party ruling at the Centre. Secondly, the discretionary powers of the Governor to invite a leader to form the Government is an arena which has hitherto attracted an unending acrimonious debate. Thirdly, the role of Governor as an agent of political party at the Centre to recommend President's rule under Article 356 of the Constitution has all along been the subject of much criticism and debate. It is the Governor's report regarding breakdown of Constitutional machinery in the State which precipitates the dismissal of an elected government. Obviously, such an exercise of power can not remain without attracting probing eyes from the parties, the press and the people. If we look into the past we would find that the matter relating to appointment of Governor was keenly debated in the Constituent Assembly. Mr. B.N. Rau, the Constitutional Advisor had submitted an independent memorandum to the Provincial Constitution Committee on May 30, 1947 suggesting that Governor should be elected by the Provincial Legislature by a secret vote according to the system of proportional representation by the single transferable vote. The Provincial Constitution Committee, headed by Sardar Patel, submitted its report to the Constituent Assembly on 15th July 1947 recommending that for each Province there shall be a Governor to be elected directly by the people on the basis of adult suffrage. Initially Constituent Assembly had accepted the idea of elected Governor and dropped the proposal of Governor nominated by the President. Govind Ballabh Pant said that the idea of nominated Governor by the President of India would be an "embarrassing duties" as he would be the President of a Federal State and should not be seen as doing anything which may raise controversy. However, an abrupt change in the political contours of the country due to Partition, underlined the need for a "strong centre" and Constituent Assembly reversed its decision by incorporating provisions for nominated Governor. Pandit Nehru told Constituent Assembly that it would be much better that Governor is nominated and thus cut away from the party politics of the Province so that the competition or the race between the rival groups is conducted in a fair, reasonable and constitutional manner. In the wake of Bommai's case and Sarkaria Commission's report, a convention was adopted whereby a consultation with Chief Minister of the State was made a precondition for appointment of Governor. It was also decided that a person to be nominated as Governor for a State should not belong to it.

The misuse of office of Governor for narrow political ends has drawn lot of political controversies. It has been used not only for the purpose of toppling the non-Congress governments but also for keeping the Assembly in suspended animation in order to enable the Congress Party to form Government by encouraging defections. There are numerous instances for such misuse. For example, in Rajasthan when the elections were held in 1967, none of the parties had an absolute majority in the Assembly, but the Congress party happened to be the largest having 88 seats out of 183. The Governor invited Mohan Lal Sukhadia to form the government on the ground that he was the leader of the largest party in the Assembly. He could not secure majority and efforts to engineer defection could not succeed. But Governor, instead of allowing leader of opposition to explore such possibility, recommended imposition of President's rule with suspension of Assembly. Similarly in Orissa in 1971 when elections were held, none of the parties had an absolute majority. But the Congress, with 51 seats out of 140, was the largest political party. Dr. Hare Krishna Mehtab was keen on forming the Government. But the Governor did not invite him to do so because he was not satisfied about majority support in the Assembly. Hence, he recommended the extension of President's rule along with suspension of Assembly.

Whenever the government of Congress party or a Government supported by it from outside or a Government in which it was a major partner, fell or was about to fall, the Assemblies were immediately dissolved to prevent non-Congress parties from trying to form government under Article 174(2). This was done in Kerala in 1970, in West Bengal and Bihar in 1971, in Orissa in 1973, in Haryana, UP and Madhya Pradesh in 1967 and in Bihar in 1969.

Now a systematic attempt is being made to shift the focus from the role of Governor to the role of Supreme Court. The whole controversy is being presented in a manner so as to reflect the whole issue as Judiciary versus Legislature. No one has convincingly explained to the nation as to how advancing the date of trial of strength can be described as an affront to the inherent powers or jurisdiction of the legislature. Nothing was explained as to why trial of strength should not be free from scope of horse-trading to which our political system is highly vulnerable. The point as to why a long duration was allowed by the Governor for trial of strength has also not been allowed to come up for debate. Similarly, what was the point over which a Presidential reference under Article 143 could be initiated except to indirectly or euphemistically tell the apex court to mind its business and to remain a mere spectator to the game of disrobing of democracy. If the situation like this is allowed to prevail, then the country would be heading towards chaos, anarchy and political instability marked by subversion of all political norms and democratic values enshrined in our Constitution. It is travesty of the whole matter that the controversy over the office of Governor has been going on since the coming into force of the Constitution but no attempt has ever been made to think over some alternative arrangement or bring about some reforms. In a quasi-federal system like that of ours, the removal of the office of Governor altogether may not be considered as a sound proposition. The question about who will summon, prorogue and dissolve the Assembly in the absence of Governor, the question of accountability particularly when the State undergoes instability and issue of ordinance, notification and above all to act as a bridge between Centre and State would then be other aspects to be dealt with. Hence removal of the post of Governor may not find favour with experts and the people. Framers of our Constitution had discussed various methods of selecting the Governor and these included: (i) election by adult suffrage, (ii) election by the members of the Lower House or both Houses of the State Legislature either by the system of proportional representation or otherwise, (iii) selection by the President our of a panel submitted by the Lower House of the State legislature, and

(iv) appointment by the President. In America, the states do not face such controversies because Governors are elected through an electoral suffrage. If some reforms are introduced in the method of appointment of Governor, the charge of politicization of the gubernatorial post can be minimized.

The role of Governor in inviting a leader to form government has all along been the subject of criticism and sometime even litigation. Article 164 of our Constitution states that the Chief Minister shall be appointed by the Governor and the other Ministers shall hold office during the pleasure of the Governor. Thus the provision which confers discretionary powers, leaves enough scope for the Governor to decide as to who should be invited to form the Government. This becomes all the more vulnerable when no party secures absolute majority in the election. The well established convention that either the single largest party or the single largest poll alliance should be invited to form the Government has also been subjected to frequent violation as witnessed during recent happenings.

In an unprecedented move, Supreme Court's Constitution Bench while delivering its judgment on January 23, 2006, held the Presidential proclamation of dissolution of Bihar Assembly as null and void. Pronouncing its historic verdict in *Rameshwar Prasad* vs. *Union of India*, Supreme Court went to the extent of accusing the Governor of misleading the Union Council of Ministers with a fiction of report on horse-trading as a grave threat to democracy. It held that overnight meeting of Cabinet and obtaining signatures on the proclamation from the President who was in Moscow on the night of May 23, 2005, was an unconstitutional move to prevent Nitish Kumar who was to stake his claim to form the Government at the dawn of May 24. On the question whether President has power to dissolve an assembly which has not met even once after February 2005 elections and whose members had not taken oath, Supreme Court took the view that there is no restriction under Article 174(2)(b) of the Constitution. The judgment came as a political tremor shaking the ruling UPA coalition Government. NDA leaders demanded the resignation of Prime Minister as it was he who presided over the Cabinet taking decision to strike a midnight coup on the democratically elected institution. Buta Singh had to fax his resignation letter. The country once again witnessed a Constitutional debate with all political bitterness. The Constitutional experts like Soli Sorabjee, Subhash Kashyap, F.S. Nariman and Shanti Bhushan were all vocal in criticizing the Central Government for blatant misuse of office of Governor for furthering political ends. Subhash Kashyap opined that it was the Central Government which did the Constitutional impropriety and Buta Singh was just made the scapegoat. Soli Sorabjee, in his article "Democracy Derailed" (the *Hindustan Times*, 3rd February 2006) wrote that it needs to be emphasized that there was no explanation whatsoever tendered before the Court about undue haste for the midnight dissolution of the assembly. Would Bihar have gone up in flames if Nitish Kumar was allowed to stake his claim, he argued. Would democracy have suffered an instant demise if the dissolution was not ordered immediately? He questioned. It would be the height of naivety to believe that the indecent haste of midnight dissolution was to save democracy in Bihar.

Since this flaw in our system is taking an ugliest shape to erode democratic norms, it would be the need of the hour to consider ways and means to bring about such reforms as are necessary to put an end to such controversies. These have led to the decline of Parliamentary system. The best course would be to introduce a provision in the Constitution that whenever a situation arises in which no political party or a pre-poll alliance gets a clear majority, then the task of ascertaining the whole political situation shall be entrusted to either the Chief Justice of the High Court of the State concerned or any panel comprising non-political persons. It should be on the basis of the advice of such a non-political panel that a Governor can invite a leader to form the Government. This will apply some checks on the biased approach in the task of formation of the government.

14

Presidential System as Panacea for Political Ills

The Presidential form of Government was initially favoured by most of the members of the Constituent Assembly. It received a highly articulated debate from all sections. Speaking before the Assembly about the form of government, Dr. B.R. Ambedkar remarked that the Draft Constitution in recommending the Parliamentary system of government has preferred more responsibility to more stability. Both systems are democratic and the choice between the two is not very easy. A democratic executive must satisfy two conditions—(1) it must be stable executive and (2) it must be responsible executive. Unfortunately it has not been possible to devise a system which can ensure both in equal degree. You can have a system which can give you more stability but less responsibility or you can have a system which gives you more responsibility but less stability. The American and Swiss systems give you more stability but less responsibility. The British system, on the other hand, gives you more responsibility but less stability.

However, his views on the form of government received flak from several members of the Assembly. He was vehemently criticised by Maulana Hasrat Mohani, a renowned Constitutionalist when he remarked—"Look at our Constitution drafted by Dr. Ambedkar. There is nothing new in it. He has mostly copied out either the government of India Act 1935 or as admitted by himself has drawn from the Constitutions of other countries. A bit from here and a bit from there—it is a Pandora Box" (*Constituent Assembly Debates*, Vol. 7, p. 45).

Another member M.A. Beg spoke that in a Parliamentary system, a Government is formed and remains saddled so long as it carries the confidence of the Parliament. But take the case of a certain section of the Parliament not being satisfied with the executive but unable to throw out the Government. It is no doubt that members of the Parliament are elected and the leader of the majority party is called by the Head of the State to form Government. It is the leader who chooses his own ministers. Upto the stage of the return of the members to Parliament, it is democratic. From that stage, it ceases to be democratic, for the leader of the majority party may choose anyone he pleases.

An inquest into five decades working of Parliamentary system in India, as discussed in preceding chapters, would lead to the conclusion that it has not lived upto the expectations initially reposed in it. The apprehensions raised in the Constituent Assembly have come to prove. Its authority is declining and it is fast succumbing to the ways of government and bureaucracy. While its work-load is increasing, its number of sittings are getting reduced. The political events followed by judicial intervention at various stages have together brought into spotlight the ludicrous failure and hollowness in the system. It is in the shadow of such a grim scenario that people are getting restive to see the light at the end of tunnel. Can Presidential system of Government which is successfully working in more than 20 countries including USA provide an answer to the political ills of the country is a question which needs to be addressed. After all it was the system which was initially accepted by most of the founding fathers of the Constitution. Montesquieu in his *Spirit of the Laws* convincingly expounded the view that the concentration of more than one type of governmental function in the hands of individual or one group of individuals leads to despotic abuse of authority and endangers the liberty of citizens.

A comparative analysis of working of Parliamentary and Presidential system in various countries would definitely take us to form an opinion that the latter would be the only system which can provide panacea to the present political ills. The fact that India is a vast heterogenous country inhabiting conglomeration of groups and communities practising different religious, precepts, cultures and languages makes it all the more necessary to switch over to this model. As the President would no longer be dependent upon the majority support in the legislative, the malpractices like forging or breaking of pre-poll or post-poll defection or intriguing politics would be curbed. While the stability of the political system would be assured, the doctrine of separation of powers coupled with provisions of checks and balances would eradicate the scope of arbitrary use of powers. His election through electoral college on the US pattern would put an end to the practice of vote bank politics. For him the whole country would be one constituency. Whatever he will speak or do, would be in keeping with the whole country and not the constituency or district or the community to which he belongs. His election from the whole country as one constituency leaves no scope for secret parleys, forging of groups, alliances or intriguing politics to install or bring down a government as we see in the Parliamentary system. It were these unique features which led Ogg and Ray to remark that "American Constitution is a document with long life but brief biography."

Attributes which strike dividing lines between Presidential and Parliamentary system can be discussed as follows:

1. Separation of Powers among Executive, Legislative and Judiciary with Checks and balances is a principle sine qua non for a Presidential form of Government. It works on the doctrine that power should be a check to power. However, in contrast, Parliamentary system envisages the accountability of executive before Parliament. It is drawn from Parliament, dependent upon Parliament for survival, accountable to Parliament and has to constantly enjoy its confidence. Parliament has power to overthrow the Government by passing a motion of non-confidence. In Presidential system on the other hand, head of the

executive, i.e. the President is neither the creation of legislature, nor part of it nor is supposed to win its confidence for survival and nor accountable to it. State powers are distributed among three organs, i.e. Executive, Legislature and Judiciary in such a manner that there can not be any stalemate or deadlock. It does not envisage a situation which may lead to complete severance in the three organs of Government. That is why the system has been successfully working in the United States for more than 200 years and in other countries for several decade together. The words like, "defection", "minorityism", "vote bank politics", "alliances", "instability", "horsetrading", etc. are not to be used and are in fact anathema to their political culture.

2. While a Prime Minister in a Parliamentary system has to be the leader of the majority party or coalition of parties and has to solicit their persistent support, the President in the Presidential system carries no such obligation and he is not to cobble up or lobby for political support from major to minor or communal to regional political parties. If Presidential system of Government is adopted in India, it would wholly alter the enter political scenario as impulsive sectarian or communal feelings would evaporate and pave the way for higher national issues. President being head of the executive elected by the whole country as one electoral body would be free from the influence of such political parties and can chalk out the plans keeping the interest of the whole country as uppermost rather than to be seen as playing galaxy to the vested interests or regional aspirations for some political pressure groups. Assured of his political survival on the country as a whole instead of few political parties pursuing their narrow interests, it would be easier for the President to resist temptations of pursuing narrow political ends.

3. The legislature in Presidential system would not have to carry the burden of electing the executive and then to support it for survival. It would thus be freed from lobbyism and behind-the-curtain corrupt practices, defection, forging of alliances, secret pacts, underground bargainings and members vying for getting ministerial berths. Loyalties would no longer be on sale. Legislatures would mean business confining its entire activities to seriously debate issues, legislate on the matters involving interest of the teeming masses. The system of checks and balances would confer upon the legislature various ways to control the executive. Its control over finance, its powers to legislate on the enumerated subjects would confer upon it a dignified aura the like of which is totally withered away in reference to the Parliament.
4. The Presidential system, wherever it is adopted, has promoted emergence of two parties system which is just opposite in the case of Parliamentary system. In India there are more than 753 political parties registered with Election Commission of India and their number is likely to swell further in the coming times. Unlike political parties in USA which fight elections on broader issues like foreign policies, political parties in India thrive on issues like poverty, ignorance, caste, religions and minority appeasements. Realising that a party having smallest number of MPs or MLAs can dictate its terms to seek pound of flesh in formation of a Government, the importance of regional parties has vastly increased in the preceding years. Regardless of their minor characters with handful representations, they dominate the political events only because survival of the government often depend upon their support. When Lok Sabha was debating over the motion of confidence moved by Shri Atal Behari Vajpayee, the then Prime Minister in 1998, few hours of delay in

getting letter of support from Ms. Jayalalitha, leader of AIADMK was sufficient to cause ripple in the whole political scenario. All ideological differences take a backseat when it comes to sharing of power.

In sharp contrast to the multi-party system which thrives in the Parliamentary system of government, the conduct and behaviour of political parties in Presidential systems is entirely different. The political equations under the Presidential system acquire such overtones that it becomes practically difficult or rather meaningless to find unbridled growth of political parties. In USA, there are two main rival parties namely Republican Party and Democratic Party. Though there are some minor parties as well but they can not acquire the political niche in the same manner as the minor parties acquire in parliamentary system. The parties like Prohibition Party, the Socialist party and the Communist Party, etc. do exist in American political system. Their programmes and activities are vast and varied. The Prohibition Party, set up in 1872 with the programme of opposing sale of liquor and policies relating to overall upliftment of the people could not come even nearer to the national parties. Similarly, Socialist Party of America has a clear programme which include public ownership of rail roads, telegraphs, telephones state ownership of mines, forests and other natural resources. It pleads for termination of the power of judicial review, abolition of Senate and election of judges. If the party has hardly any dominating role it is because of the fact that no government is dependent upon their strength in legislature for survival. The Communist Party, which is a well organised party deriving support from some sections of working class, too could not acquire the national status. It is difficult for a political party to reach to the centre stage by representing few or limited section of society. A clear inference can thus

> be drawn that multi-party system with all its vices and wickedness, flourishes only in Parliamentary system where they acquire bargaining capacity to get loaves and fishes of offices by bartering their minority support to an otherwise weak and tottering government. It leads to instability, corruption and uncertainty fuelling all sorts of speculations. In presidential system, however, such a phenomenon is non-existent as no political party thriving on regional, caste or sectarian appeal can spread its wings by mere extending support to or withdrawing support from a coalition government.

Lord Bryce who conducted an indepth analytical study of American two Parties, likened them to two bottles each having label denoting the kinds of liquor it contained but both were in fact empty. He said this because there is hardly anything distinguishable between the political and economic policies of the two parties. They have hardly any commitment to a particular ideology, dogma, or set of programmes which can draw a parallel line between the two parties. Both uphold liberal approach towards capitalism and both adopt the same approach to tackle the internal problems. It is predominantly the fall out of foreign policies which casts its spell on electoral issues. The Democrats espouse the interests of peasants and favour continuation of slavery. Republicans represent the industrial cases and so they sought its abolition. But these issues have not been blown out of proportion to create any sharp wedge between the two parties. According to Finer—"America has only one party, Republican cum Democratic divided into nearly equal halves by habits and the contests for office; the Republican bearing one half and the Democratic being the other half of the party." America being a highly industrialized, progressive and prosperous country is competent to repel rhetoricism of fervent appeals of political parties.

Separation of powers between Executive, Legislature and Judiciary with system of checks and balance is the cardinal principle of the Presidential form of Government. It stands on the premise that accumulation of powers in one person or one organ unleashes tyrannical governance and separation of powers is the only perfect way out in the direction to set up a truly democratic political system. Wherever there is concentration of power, there can not remain liberty, fraternity and equality without being infringed. James Madison wrote in Federalist "No political truth is certainly of greater intrinsic value than that the accumulation of all powers, legislature, executive and judiciary in the same hands may justly be pronounced the very definition of tyranny." The American constitution does not make out a direct declaration using separation of power as a Constitutional phrase. Yet it introduces the system by dealing the three organs legislature, executive and judiciary separately. It works on the principle that power should be a check to power. Since a complete separation among these organs can not be a sound political proposition, it makes a harmonious balance in such a manner that no organ enters into others' field or usurp others' powers in any form or manner whatsoever. It is this unique blend of separation or powers with effective check and balance and harmony which led Frederic Ogg to remark—"No feature of American government national, state and often local is more characteristic than the separation of powers combined with precautionary checks and balances." A separation of powers devoid of checks and balances would end up in chaos and conflict and such a system can not augur well for setting up a Presidential form of Government. A separation can not be at the cost of equilibrium and harmony among the three organs.

A peripherial view of 230 years long working of American Constitution is bound to leave an indelible impression on the mind of any Constitutionalist forcing him to ponder how it would have survived events of crisis, turbulence and upheavals. It gives President the power to appoint officers of his choice but such appointments have to be approved by Senate, the upper house of Congress the legislature. President appoints judges of the Supreme Court. But such appointments have to be approved by Senate. Similarly, President has power to negotiate with foreign countries and enter into treaties or agreement with them. But all such treaties are subject to ratification of Senate. The power to ratify or refuse to ratify a treaty signed by President has been used freely by the Senate. In 1919, Senate refused to ratify the Treaty of Versailles which was accepted by President Woodrow Wilson. Under the Constitution, President is Commander-in-Chief of the army. But power to declare war is with Congress. However, President may through the conduct of foreign affairs of the country bring about a situation which may ultimately lead to the war leaving no option for Congress to take any other decision. President Mckinely despatched a battleship to Havana which ultimately led to war with Spain. Whenever country remained in wars, President enjoyed vast powers in foreign affairs. Similarly, Congress which enjoys legislative powers is not absolutely free to legislate on any matter in an unbridled manner. Bills passed by Congress must be submitted to President for his approval. He may veto a Bill. But even this power of veto can not be used in an unrestrained manner as Congress can override it by repassing the Bill with two-thirds majority voting separately in two houses. The President has abused the right to veto the Bill in various manners. This has been on both political and non-political reasons. The Republican have held the majority position in both Houses since the election of 1994, except for a brief period from 2001 to 2003 when the Democrats were in majority in Senate. Prior to that, the Democratic party was in majority in both the Houses of Congress for a major period since 1954. Similarly, judiciary exercises its control over Executive and the Congress through its power of judicial review.

Since Executive is not a part of the legislature, any member of either House may introduce Bills himself or at the behest of lobbyists or Pressure groups which are legally required to be registered in a Central database. Each Bill goes through several stages and the first stage involves consideration by a Committee. Most of the Bills are deliberated upon by Standing Committees, each of which has jurisdiction over a particular subject matter. On the basis of reports of the Committee, the Bill reaches the floor of the House. The House may debate and amend the Bill. Members of House of Representation and Senate are not under strict control or discipline of the political parties as we see in Parliamentary system where whip system is capable enough to create a binding obligation on the member. Leaders of political parties in America do not have power to issue a mandatory instruction on their members. Nevertheless they have certain powers to sway reluctant legislators to vote with the party. Once a Bill is approved by one House, it is sent to the other, which may pass, reject or amend it. In order for the Bill to become law, both the Houses must agree to the version of the Bill. If Senate, the upper House makes any amendment in the Bill, the amended version has to be referred to a Conference Committee for reconciling the two versions. When the reconciled Bill is passed by both the Houses, it is submitted to the President. The President, if accords his assent to the Bill, it becomes a law. If, however, President chooses to veto the Bill, or returns it to Congress with his observation, the Bill can become law only if each House of Congress votes with two-thirds members again to override the veto. This is how system of checks and balances functions in so far as the working of two organs, i.e. President and the Congress.

The third organ, i.e. the judiciary occupies a dominant position in the realm of entire constitutional set up. Though it enjoys a considerable amount of independence with all judicial powers, it is nevertheless a part of the system of checks and balance. While the President appoints the judges of the Supreme Court, the Congress determines their number and fixes their salaries as well. Moreover, all such appointments by the Presidents are subject to the approval of the Senate. Once appointed and assumed the offices, the judges can not be controlled either by Congress or by the President. A judge can be removed only through impeachment process which is not an ordinary course to follow. Supreme Court while exercising power of judicial review and implied powers under "due process of law", is competent to declare any law or executive order as unconstitutional and ultravires which means, in effect, they become null and void and can not be enforced.

Dr. R. Venkataraman, former President of India, while delivering a lecture on 16th October, 1999 at India International Centre on subject "Stable Government of India", came down heavily upon the stinking political system prevalent in the country. He openly advocated for switching over to Presidential form of government. His views as stated below were widely acclaimed and Constitutional expert had endorsed them.

In a multi-party system, parties can unite for bringing down the government but may not agree on a successor government as happened in our country recently. The rule envisaged will prevent reckless wrecking of governments.

This reform alone cannot resolve all the political maladies that afflict our nation. The bane of small parties wrecking the government may be reduced but not eliminated under the reform referred to above. We will have to examine other alternatives for securing a stable government for the nation.

India on becoming independent deliberately chose the Westminster type of parliamentary democracy. Most of the leaders of the struggle for freedom were from the legal profession with skills to match the foreign government in knowledge and debate. Many among them have had their education, general and legal, in England and had imbibed the liberal traditions of Mill and Laski. Besides, Britain, in their days was a super-power spread over the entire globe and as it used to be said, "the sun never sets in the British Empire." Authors and pandits extolled the British Parliamentary system so profusely that it appealed to many intellectuals in the world as an unerring model for others to follow. Ivor Jennings described the British constitution as one of the strongest, if not the strongest, in the world. Dr. K.M. Munshi, one of the architects of our constitution, summed up the prevalent thinking at the time in his speech in the Constitution Assembly:

> Most of us and during the last several generation before us, public men in India, have looked up to the British model as the best. For the last thirty or forty years, some kind of responsibility has been introduced in the governance of this country. After

> this experience, why should we go back on the tradition that has been built for over 100 years.

No wonder, we adopted the Westminster type of parliamentary democracy, with the addition of a few chapters such as Fundamental Rights and Directive Principles of State Policy, etc.

During the first decade, when the stalwarts of the Freedom movement brewed in selfless dedication, service and sacrifice held sway of the country. India functioned as a mature democracy and elicited the admiration of the entire world including that of the sceptics who doubted the chances of adult franchise working satisfactorily among unlettered people. In international conferences and meetings we were heard with respect and attention. Our felicity of expression in the international language, namely English, gave us an added advantage over others. That decade provided stability and growth to the Central and State Governments.

Thereafter several weaknesses and flaws in the functioning of our democracy surfaced throughout the country, casting considerable doubt over the stability and strength of the State and Central Governments. In Kerala, the Congress Ministry was defeated by defection of Congress members themselves. In Congress legislature parties, dissident groups developed, threatening the Ministry every now and then. Government were engaged more in their survival rather than in service of the people. Mushroom parties unable to provide a viable alternative government sprang up every other day. Multi-party system was found incompatible with the Westminster type of democracy based on Two-Party system.

I therefore, fired the first salvo against the Cabinet Form in 1965 by sending a resolution to the All India Congress Committee (AICC) asking for the constitution of a Committee to examine and report:

> Whether the present Cabinet form of Government at the Centre and the states may be replaced by an executive directly elected by the people for a fixed term of years and if so to recommend consequential changes in the Constitution of India as appropriate.

The Westminster pattern of Parliamentary Democracy has succeeded only in countries like Australia, Canada, and New Zealand, apart from Britain, all of which have a sound two-party system. Despite centuries, these countries and the United States have had strong two parties so that one or the other party represents the majority of the nation in a general election. On the other hand, parties in India split overnight and the number of parties goes on increasing instead of reducing. I said at that time that,

> The hope that in a multi-party system, dependence on one or more small groups will become necessary to form government seems to encourage the formation of smaller groups in the legislature. These groups expect that they will be able to hold balance of power and obtain bargaining strength. (Vide *The Presidential System* by A.G. Noorani, p. 30)

Two-Party System

The Westminster type of Parliamentary Democracy on which our Constitution has been modeled has many attractive features. The Prime Minister, being the leader of the majority party in Parliament, is able, unlike the American President, to carry out his policies and programs without any hindrance. Besides the chances of conflict between the legislature and the executive are minimal. Furthermore, Executive's accountability to Parliament is total and the continuance of the government itself depends on the support of the majority in Parliament. However, if the major parties, Conservative and Labour, split into two each, all tangles which plague Indian Parliament will be re-enacted in Britain also. Ivor Jennings dealing with prerogative of the Crown to decline the Prime Minister's advice for dissolution of the House in limited cases in his book *Cabinet Government* (3rd edition pp. 427-28) has said that while the Queen's personal prerogative to dissolve the House is maintained in theory, there are hardly any circumstances in which it could be exercised in practice. He added that this assumed a continuance of the two-party system. "If major parties break up, the whole balance of the constitution alters and then possibly the Queen's prerogative becomes important.

(Vide *Constitutional and Administrative Law,* 7th Edition by Hood Philips, pp. 154-55).

Ivor Jennings himself concedes that the British model is based on a two-party system and the whole balance of the British Constitution will change if the major parties in Britain break up like ours.

Therefore, if the present Constitution is to function satisfactorily two reforms—change in the electoral system and de-recognition of more than two political parties—are indispensable."

The Constitution of United States of America—Its Rigidity as Salient Feature and Impact on System

For a Presidential form of government to succeed, it is essential that Constitution should be rigid so as to enable all organs of the Government to work in tandem without in any manner eroding its substance. If the Constitution is flexible, an organ of the Government may try to misuse the power to amend the Constitution thereby disturbing the equilibrium in distribution of powers. Separation of powers under the Constitution must be so devised that no organ should contemplate of usurping the powers bestowed on other organ. This can be possible only if the procedure of amendment in the Constitution is made complex and rigid. An analytical study of the working of all Presidential systems in various countries would establish that such a system would not have survived in the event of flexible constitution. If we take into account the American Constitution which has a long chequered history of more than the two centuries, hardly 27 Amendments have been introduced. It is the oldest written Constitution in existence and the shortest of the constitutions of any other nation. Containing only 4000 words, it is a fine, evenly balanced and yet a rigid charter laying down the rules of government organs and rights of citizens under a democratic system. It was drafted during a two months marathon debate in a highly guarded convention at Philadelphia. The men who chartered the destiny of their country were renowned thinkers, Constitutional experts and patriots and included George Washington, James Madisons, Alexander Hamilton, Benjamin Franklin, James

Wilson and others. None of the portion of debates was leaked. Yet the Draft was sent for ratification by all the States. Its rigidity is principled and does not betray signs of obsessive morbidity.

Giving full credence to the future shape of things and recognizing the change being law of nature, the authors of American Constitution made provision for amendment in the Constitution so that it may remain a dynamic one to suit to the changes which commonly take place with the passage of time. Article V of the Constitution provides:

> The Congress whenever two-thirds of both Houses shall propose amendments to this Constitution, or on the application of the Legislatures of two-thirds of the several States, shall call a convention for proposing amendments, which, in either case, shall be valid to all intents and purposes, as part of this Constitution, when ratified by the legislatures of three-fourths of the several states, or by conventions by three-fourths thereof, as the one or the other mode of ratification may be proposed by the Congress, provided that no amendment which may be made prior to the year one thousand eight hundred and eight shall in any manner affect the first and fourth clauses in the ninth section of the first article, and that no state, without its consent, shall be deprived of its equal suffrage in the Senate.

In the whole process of amendment, neither the President of America nor Governors of States have any role to play. As amendment is held to be solely a legislative function, President or the Governors are not to sign the Amendment or instruments of ratification. A state legislative which has ratified an amendment, can not subsequently withdraw its ratification. But a State legislature may refuse to ratify it and after such refusal can reconsider and then ratify it notwithstanding its earlier refusal. No time limit is fixed for ratification. The amendment can be proposed by two-thirds votes of the two houses of Congress. The same can be proposed on the petition of two-thirds, i.e. 34 of the states also. However, every such amendment shall have to be ratified by the legislatures of three-fourths, i.e. 38 States or by Conventions in three-fourths of the States. The amendment procedure is thus so cumbersome, complex and circuitous that out of thousands of resolutions seeking amendments only 27 could succeed during the long span of more than two centuries. The absence of time limit for ratification is another factor which comes as a stumbling block before any amendment is set in motion. On one occasion, Ohio state ratified an amendment 80 years after it was referred to it. A state can refer an Amendment to the people of the State for eliciting their opinion. But it can not abdicate its own powers and is free to take a final view after eliciting the opinion of the people. Getting two-thirds majority in Congress and then three-fourths States for ratification is by itself a stupendous job to undertake and see the whole process completed in life time.

A brief look to the Amendments that have hitherto introduced and adopted would reveal the Americans' wisdom and state of vigilance to their rights. The amendments were over matters like freedom of speech, slavery and involuntary servitude, right to vote without race, colour or condition of servitude and restricting the terms for the President, etc.

Amendment I

Congress shall make no law respecting an establishment of religion, or prohibiting the free exercise thereof; or abridging the freedom of speech, or of the press; or the right of the people peaceably to assemble, and to petition the Government for a redress of grievances.

The first ten amendments were passed by Congress on 25 September 1789 and were ratified by three-fourths of the States on 15 December 1791.

Amendment II

A well regulated Militia, being necessary to the security of a free State, the right of the people to keep and bear Arms shall not be infringed.

Amendment III

No soldier shall, in time of peace, be quartered in any house, without the consent of the Owner, nor in time of war, but in a manner to be prescribed by law.

Amendment IV

The right of the people to be secure in their persons, houses, papers, and effects, against unreasonable searches and seizures, shall not be violated, and no Warrants shall issue, but upon probable cause, supported by Oath or affirmation and particularly describing the place to be searched and the persons or things to be seized.

Amendment V

No person shall be held to answer for a capital or otherwise infamours crime, unless on a presentment or indictment of a Grand Jury, except in cases arising in the land or naval forces, or in the Militia, when in actual service in time of War or public danger; nor shall any person be subject for the same offence to be twice put in jeopardy of life or limb; nor shall be compelled in any criminal case to be a witness against himself, nor be deprived of life, liberty, or property, without due process of law; nor shall private property be taken for public use, without just compensation.

Amendment VI

In all criminal prosecutions, the accused shall enjoy the right to a speedy and public trial, by an impartial jury of the State and district wherein the crime shall have been committed, which district shall have been previously ascertained by law, and to be informed of the nature and cause of the accusation; to be confronted with the witnesses against him; to have compulsory process for obtaining witnesses in his favor and to have the Assistance of Counsel for his defence.

Amendment VII

In suits at common law, where the value in controversy shall exceed twenty dollars, the right of trial by jury shall be preserved, and no fact tried by a jury, shall be otherwise re-examined in any Court of the United States, than according to the rules of the common law.

Amendment VIII

Excessive bail shall not be required, nor excessive fines imposed, nor cruel and unusual punishments inflicted.

Amendment IX

The enumeration in the Constitution, of certain rights, shall not be construed to deny or disparage others retained by the people.

Amendment X

The powers not delegated to the United States by the Constitution, nor prohibited by it to the States, are reserved to the States respectively, or to the people.

Amendment XI

The Judicial power of the United States shall not be construed to extend to any suit in law or equity, commenced or prosecuted against one of the United States by Citizens of another State, or by Citizens or Subjects of any Foreign State.

Amendment XII

The Electors shall meet in their respective States and vote by ballot for President and Vice President, one of whom, at least, shall not be an inhabitant of the same State with themselves; they shall name in their ballots the person voted for as President, and in distinct ballots the person voted for as Vice President, and they shall make distinct lists of all persons voted for as President, and of all persons voted for as Vice President, and of the number of votes for each, which lists they shall sign and certify, and transmit sealed to the seat of the government of the United States, directed to the President of the Senate;—The President of the Senate shall, in the presence of the Senate and House of Representatives, open all the certificates and the votes shall then be counted;—The person having the greatest number of votes for President, shall be the President, if such number be a majority of the whole number of Electors appointed; and if no person have such majority, then from the persons having the highest numbers not exceeding three on the list of those voted for as President, the House of Representatives shall choose immediately, by ballot, the President. But in choosing the President, the votes shall be taken by States, the representation from each state having one vote; a quorum for this purpose shall consist of a member or members from two-thirds of the states, and a majority of all the states shall be necessary to a choice. And if the House of Representatives shall not choose a President whenever the right of choice shall devolve upon them, before the fourth day of March next following, then the Vice President shall act as President, as in the case of the death or other constitutional disability of the President. The person having the greatest number of votes as Vice President, shall be the Vice President, if such number be a majority of the whole number of Electors appointed, and if no person have a majority, then from the two highest numbers on the list, the Senate shall choose the Vice President; a quorum for the purpose shall consist of two-thirds of the whole number of Senators, and a majority of the whole number shall be necessary to a choice. But no person constitutionally ineligible to the office of President shall be eligible to that of Vice President of the United States.

Amendment XIII

Neither slavery nor involuntary servitude, except as a punishment for crime whereof the party shall have been duly convicted, shall exist within the United States, or any place subject to their jurisdiction. Congress shall have power to enforce this article by appropriate legislation.

Amendment XIV

All persons born or naturalized in the United States, and subject to the jurisdiction thereof, are citizens of the United States and of the State wherein they reside. No State shall make or enforce any law which shall abridge the privileges or immunities of citizens of the United States; nor shall any State deprive any person of life, liberty, or property, without due process of law; nor deny to any person within its jurisdiction the equal protection of the laws.

Representatives shall be apportioned among the several States according to their respective numbers, counting the whole number of persons in each State, excluding Indians not taxed. But when the right to vote at any election for the choice of electors for President and Vice President of the United States, Representatives in Congress, the Executive and Judicial officers of a State, or the members of the Legislature thereof, is denied to any of the male inhabitants of such State, being twenty-one years of age, and citizens of the United States, or in any way abridged, except for participation in rebellion, or other crime, the basis of representation therein shall be reduced in the proportion which the number of such male citizens shall bear to the whole number of male citizens twenty-one years of age in such State. No person shall be a Senator or Representative in Congress, or elector of President and Vice President, or hold any office, civil or military, under the United States, or under any State, who having previously taken an oath, as member of Congress, or as an officer of the United States, or as a member of any State legislature, or as an executive or judicial officer of any State, to support the Constitution of the United States, shall have engaged in insurrection or rebellion against the same, or given aid or comfort to the enemies thereof. But Congress may by a vote of two-thirds of each House, remove such disability.

The validity of the public debt of the United States, authorized by law, including debts incurred for payment of pensions and bounties for services in suppressing insurrection or rebellion, shall not be questioned. But neither the United States nor any State shall assume or pay any debt or obligation incurred in aid of insurrection or rebellion against the United States, or any claim for the loss or emancipation of any slave; but all such debts, obligations and claim shall be held illegal and void.

The Congress shall have the power to enforce, by appropriate legislation, the provisions of this article.

Amendment XV (Negro Suffrage)

The right of citizens of the United States to vote shall not be denied or abridged by the United States or by any State on account of race, color, or previous condition of servitude. The Congress shall have power to enforce this article by appropriate legislation.

Amendment XVI

The Congress shall have power to lay and collect taxes on incomes from whatever source derived, without apportionment among the several States and without regard to any census or enumeration.

Amendment XVII

The Senate of the United States shall be composed of two Senators from each State, elected by the people thereof, for six years; and each Senator shall have one vote. The electors in each State shall have the qualifications requisite for electors of the most numerous branch of the State legislatures. When vacancies happen in the representation of any State in the Senate, the executive authority of such State shall issue writs of election to fill such vacancies; Provided that, the legislature of any State may empower the executive thereof to make temporary appointments until the people fill the vacancies by election as the legislature may direct. This amendment shall not be so construed as to affect the election or term of any Senator chosen before it becomes valid as part of the Constitution.

Amendment XVIII

Section 1. After one year from the ratification of this article the manufacture, sale, or transportation of intoxicating liquors within, the importation thereof into, or the exportation thereof from the United States and all territory subject to the jurisdiction thereof for beverage purposes is hereby prohibited.

Section 2. The Congress and the several States shall have concurrent power to enforce this article by appropriate legislation.

Section 3. This article shall be inoperative unless it shall have been ratified as an amendment to the Constitution by the legislatures of the several States, as provided in the Constitution, within seven years from the date of the submission hereof to the States by the Congress.

Amendment XIX (Woman suffrage)

The right of citizens of the United States to vote shall not be denied or abridged by the United States or by any State on account of sex.

Congress all have power to enforce this article by appropriate legislation.

Amendment XX (Inauguration)

Section 1. The terms of the President and Vice President shall end at noon on the 20th day of January, and the terms of Senators and Representatives at noon on the 3rd day of January, of the years in which such terms would have ended if this article had not been ratified; and the terms of their successors shall then begin.

Section 2. The Congress shall assemble at least once in every year and such meeting shall begin at noon on the 3rd day of January, unless they shall by law appoint a different day.

Section 3. If, at the time fixed for the beginning of the term of the President, the President elect shall have died, the Vice President elect shall become President. If a President shall not have been chosen before the time fixed for the beginning of his term, or if the President elect shall have failed to qualify, then the Vice President elect shall act as President until a President shall have qualified; and the Congress may by law provide for the case wherein neither a President elect nor a Vice President elect shall have qualified, declaring who shall then act as President, or the manner in which one who is to act shall be selected, and such person shall act accordingly until a President or Vice President shall have qualified.

Section 4. The Congress may by law provide for the case of the death of any of the persons from whom the House of Representatives may choose a President whenever the right of choice shall have devolved upon them, and for the case of the death of any of the persons from whom the Senate may choose a Vice President whenever the right of choice shall have devolved upon them.

Section 5. Sections 1 and 2 shall take effect on the 15th day of October following the ratification of this article.

Section 6. This article shall be inoperative unless it shall have been ratified as an amendment to the Constitution by the legislatures of three-fourths of the several States within seven years from the date of its submission.

Amendment XXI

Section 1. The eighteenth article of amendment to the Constitution of the United States is hereby repealed.

Section 2. The transportation or importation into any State, Territory, or possession of the United States for delivery or use therein of intoxicating liquors, in violation of the laws thereof, is hereby prohibited.

Section 3. This article shall be inoperative unless it shall have been ratified as an amendment to the Constitution by conventions in the several States, as provided in the Constitution, within seven years from the date of the submission hereof to the States by the Congress.

Amendment XXII (No third term)

No person shall be elected to the office of the President more than twice, and no person who has held the office of President, or acted as President, for more than two years of a term to which some other person was elected President shall be elected to the office of the President more than once.

But this Article shall not apply to any person holding the office of President when this Article was proposed by the Congress, and shall not prevent any person who may be holding the office of President, or acting as President, during the term within which this Article becomes operative from holding the office of President or acting as President during the remainder of such term.

Amendment XXIII

Section 1. The District constituting the seat of Government of the United States shall appoint in such manner as the Congress may direct:

> A number of electors of President and Vice President equal to the whole number of Senators and Representatives in Congress to which the District

would be entitled if it were a State, but in no event more than the least populous State; they shall be in addition to those appointed by the States, but they shall be considered, for the purposes of the election of President and Vice President, to the electors appointed by the State; and they shall meet in the District and perform such duties as provided by the twelfth article of amendment.

Section 2. The Congress shall have power to enforce this article by appropriate legislation.

Amendment XXIV

Section 1. The right of citizens of the United States to vote in any primary or other election for President or Vice President, for electors for President or Vice President, or for Senator or Representative in Congress, shall not be denied or abridged by the United States or any State by reason of failure to pay any poll tax or other tax.

Section 2. The Congress shall have power to enforce this article by appropriate legislation.

Amendment XXV (Disability)

Section 1. In case of the removal of the President from office or of his death or resignation, the Vice President shall become President.

Section 2. Whenever there is a vacancy in the office of the Vice President, the President shall nominate a Vice President who shall take office upon confirmation by a majority vote of both Houses of Congress.

Section 3. Whenever the President transmits to the President pro-tempore of the Senate and the Speaker of the House of Representatives his written declaration that he is unable to discharge the powers and duties of his office, and until he transmits to them a written declaration to the contrary, such powers and duties shall be discharged by the Vice President as Acting President.

Section 4. Whenever the Vice President and a majority of either the principal officers of the executive department or of such other body as Congress may by law provide, transmit to the President pro-tempore of the Senate and the Speaker of the House of Representatives their written declaration that the President is unable to discharge the powers and duties of his office, the Vice President shall immediately assume the powers and duties of the office as Acting President.

Thereafter, when the President transmits to the President pro-tempore of the Senate and the Speaker of the House of Representatives his written declaration that no inability exists, he shall resume the powers and duties of his office unless the Vice President and a majority of either the principal officers of the executive department or of such other body as Congress may by law provide, transmit within four days to the President pro-tempore of the Senate and the Speaker of the House of Representatives their written declaration that the President is unable to discharge the powers and duties of his office. Thereupon Congress shall decide the issue, assembling within forty-eight hours for that purpose if not in session. If the Congress, within twenty-one days after receipt of the latter written declaration, or, if Congress is not in session, within twenty-one days after Congress is required to assemble, determines by two-thirds vote of both Houses that the President is unable to discharge the powers and duties of his office, the Vice President shall continue to discharge the same as Acting President; otherwise, the President shall resume the powers and duties of his office.

Amendment XXVI

Section 1. The right of citizens of the United States, who are 18 years of age or older, to vote shall not be denied or abridged by the United States or any State on account of age.

Section 2. The Congress shall have power to enforce this article by appropriate legislation.

Amendment XXVII

No law, varying the compensation for the services of the Senators and Representatives, shall take effect, until an election of Representatives shall have intervened.

WORKING OF PRESIDENTIAL FORM OF GOVERNMENT IN DIFFERENT COUNTRIES

The Presidential form of government is working in nearly 23 countrics, viz. Argentina, Brazil, Bolivia, Chile, Colombia, Costa Rica, Cuba, Dominican Republic, El Salvador, Guatemala, Haiti, Honduras, Liberia, Mexico, Nicaragua, Panama, Paraguay, Peru, South Morea, South Vietnam, Uruguay, U.S.A. and Venezuela. However, the doctrine of separation of power has no uniform application and constitutional provisions differ from country to country. In various countries, the President possesses vast powers even in matters relating to legislature and judiciary. The Constitution of Islamic Republic of Iran was approved by a nationalist referendum in December 1979, confers vast powers on President. It gives supreme authority to the spiritual leader which position was held by Ayatollah Khomeini. Legislative power is vested in a 290 members Islamic Consultative Assembly directly elected on a non-party basis for a four year term by all citizens aged 17 years or above. No ballot papers are printed. Electors have to write the name of candidate. In the Presidential election held in June 2003, Mohammed Ahmedinezad was elected as President. Such a system can not be truly construed as a Presidential form of government because of lack of separation of power and an independent judiciary having power of judicial review vested in it.

Having discussed the Presidential form of government as prevailing in United States, we may take up the working of this system in other countries.

Working of Presidential System in Mexico

Mexico constitutional arrangement resembles those of the United States. Like the United States, it is a democratic and federal system with separation of powers and a bicameral legislature. Both the countries have their system rooted in democratic principles. Yet the President of Mexico differs in his constitutional position from his United States counterpart in several ways. The President is elected for a term of six years and is not eligible for re-election for another term. He is elected by direct, popular universal suffrage. There is no second round of counting. He must be a Mexican citizen by birth, son of either a Mexican father or mother and having resided in the country for at least 20 years. The President has the powers to make appointment of officers at top echelons, to present the Budget, to initiate and veto legislation and to command the armed forces. He can delay promulgation of a law passed by the Congress and has the power to implement legislation by decrees having the force of law. Unlike USA where Senate enjoys a dominating position in the bicameral legislature, the Senate of Mexico does not have the same power and system of checks and balance does not confer upon it the same position. Since Mexico follows a one-party system the legislature can play only a very restricted role with relation to the head of the party to which almost all its members belong.

Another significant feature which distinguishes the Mexican system from rest of the systems relates to the "President's cabinet" comprising the country's leading figure, and persons drawn from different fields. By and large, it is from this Cabinet that the next President is often chosen. The ministers of "President's Cabinet" are not answerable to the legislature nor they survive at its pleasure. The experience of the working of the "President's Cabinet" has not been found encouraging as it has promoted nepotism, corruption and hearsay politics.

Mexico is a federal state wherein States are autonomous with their own elected Governors and legislatures with a rigid constitution, the States can claim to have autonomy in their respective spheres.

Procedure for Amendment in Mexican Constitution

Like United States Constitution, the Mexican Constitution lays down an elaborate procedure for carrying out amendment in the Constitution. Title VIII Article 135 of the Constitution provides that the present Constitution may be added to or amended. In order that the addition or amendments shall become a part thereof, it shall be required that the Congress of the Union, by a vote of two-thirds of the individuals present, agree to the amendments or addition and that they be approved by a majority of the legislatures of the States. The

Congress of the Union or the Permanent Committee as the case may be, shall count the votes of the legislatures and shall announce those additions or amendments that have been approved.

In its nearly 90 years old working since 1917, the Constitution could be amended only for 59 times. The working of Presidential system in Mexico is successful as it has enabled the country to face the challenges of myriad nature and provided stability to the political set up.

Working of Presidential System in Brazil

Since 1970s, Brazil emerged as the fastest growing country in the world. Yet its people continued to be deprived of having democratic rights as it remained under the Military rule from 1964 to 1985. It was in year 1984 when Brazilian population rose as one nation to overthrow the military rule and change the Constitution. A persistent struggle by the people ultimately translated the goal of freedom into reality when on 5th October 1988 the country adopted its Constitution restoring democratic rights to the people.

The Brazilian Constitution of 1988 sets up a Presidential system of government with separation of powers among Executive headed by President, Legislature named as National Congress and an independent judiciary namely the Supreme Federal Tribunal.

The executive power is exercised by the President of the Republic, assisted by the Minister of State. He is elected for four years. The President takes office in a session of the National Congress pledging to maintain, defend and carry out the Constitution, obey the laws, promote the general well-being of the Brazilian people, sustain the Union, the integrity and the independent of Brazil. He shall have the power to appoint and dismiss the Ministers of State, exercise, with the assistance of Ministers of State, the higher management of the federal administrative sanction, promulgate and order the publication of laws, as well as to issue decrees and regulations for the true enforcement thereof, veto bills, wholly or in part, provide by means of decree on organization and structure of federal administration, in the cases where there is neither increase of expenses nor creation or extinction of public agencies, extinction of offices or positions when not held, maintain relations with forest states and conclude international treaties, conventions and acts, decree the state of defense and state of siege and exercise the supreme command of the armed forces and perform other duties as set forth in the Constitution.

Legislative power is exercised by the National Congress, which is composed of the Chamber of Deputies and the Federal Senate both have the term of four years. The Chamber of Deputies is composed by representative of the people, elected by the proportional system in each state, territory and in the Federal District. The Federal Senate is composed of representatives of the States and of the Federal District elected by a majority vote. Each state and the Federal District shall elect three Senators.

The National Congress shall have the power, with the sanction of the President of the Republic, which shall not be required for the matters specified in Articles 49, 51 and 52 to provide for all the matters within the competence of the Union and especially on the system of taxation, collection of taxes, annual budget, currency, foreign exchange, fixation of remuneration of the justices of the Supreme Federal Tribunal. It falls within the competence of the National Congress to decide on international treaties, agreements and to authorize the President of the Republic to declare war, to make peace and to permit foreign forces to pass through the national territory, to authorize the President and the Vice President of the Republic to leave the country, when such absence exceeds fifteen days, to approve a state of defense and federal intervention.

President also enjoys the power to propose amendment in the Constitution subject to the procedure as laid down in Sub-section II of the Constitution.

Amendment to the Constitution

Brazilian Constitution provides a rigid procedure for bringing out amendment in the Constitution. Article 60 of the

Constitution provides that the Constitution may be amended on the proposal of (I) at least one-third of the members of the Chamber of Deputies or of the Federal Senate, (II) the President of the Republic, and (III) more than one half of the Legislative Assemblies of the units of the Federation, each of them expressing itself by the relative majority of its members. The proposal shall be discussed and voted upon in each House of the National Congress, in two readings, and it shall be considered approved of it obtain in both readings, three-fifths of the votes of the respective members.

The amendment procedure as laid down in the Constitution creates a bar against proposal for bringing out amendment in several features, considered sacrosanct and transcendental in nature. It provides that no proposal of amendment shall be considered which is aimed at the abolishing—(I) the federative form of State, (II) the direct, secret, universal and periodic vote, (III) the separation of the Government powers, and (IV) the individual rights and guarantees. Once a proposal is rejected or considered impaired, it can not be the subject of another proposal in the same legislative session.

Since its promulgation in 1988, the Brazilian Constitution has been amended 48 times to relate to the changes in the economic order. Large monopolies in fields like petroleum, tele-communications and banking, etc. were created in favour of State-owned companies to enable them to do well for the citizens. Private banks were allowed to compete with giant State banks, but to prevent abuse, a limit of 12% p.a. was imposed to the interest rates.

Constitution of Brazil provides a bar against dynastic representation. It provides that the spouse and relative by blood or marriage upto the second degree or by adoption of the President of the Republic of the Governor of a State or Territory, or of the Federal District of a Mayor or those that have replaced them during the six months preceding the election are not eligible in the jurisdiction of the incumbent, unless they already hold an elective office and are candidates for re-election. If similar provisions with suitable modification are incorporated, the ominous trends emerging on the political horizon of the country can be thwarted successfully to salvage the system from getting murkier.

Working of Presidential System in Venezuela

The Constitution of the Bolivarian Republic of Venezuela was drafted in mid-1999 by a Constituent Assembly that was created by popular referendum. The National Constituent Assembly consisting of 131 elected individuals, was convened in August 1999 to write Constitution. The Constitution of 1999 was the first Constitution approved by popular referendum in Venezuelan history. Containing 350 Articles, the Venezuelan Constitution is world's second longest and most comprehensive document. In the same year, it was presented to people on 15th Dec 1999 and promulgated on 20th Dec 1999 after getting approval of electorate with 71.78 per cent 'yes vote'.

The politics of Venezuela takes place in a framework of a Presidential Republic whereby the President of Venezuela is both head of State and head of government. The text of the Constitution is described as an interesting hybrid of jurisprudential and political norms drawn from sources as wide as Simon Bolivar's writings on sovereignty.

Separation of powers in five Branches instead of usual three.

Instead of usual three organs of government, the new Bolivarian Republic of Venezuela has five:

(i) The Executive Branch (the President)

(ii) The Legislative Branch (the National Assembly)

(iii) The Judicial Branch (the Judiciary)

(iv) The Electoral Branch (the Electoral Power)

(v) The Citizens' Branch (the Citizen Power—Ombudsman).

The Electoral Branch is headed by the National Electoral Council (CNE) and is responsible for the independent oversight of all elections in the country, municipal, state and federal.

The Citizen Branch is constituted by the Chief Public Prosecutor and the Comptroller General. It is responsible for representing and defending the citizens in their dealings with powers of the Venezuela State.

A Strengthened and recallable presidency

It also increased the Presidential term of office from four to six years and introduced a Presidential two-term limit. The document also introduced provisions for national presidential recall referenda—that is, Venezuelan voters now were to be given the right to remove their President from office before the expiration of the Presidential term. Such referenda were to be activated upon provisions of petitions with a valid number of signatures. This new provision was brought into use in 2004 but it failed to receive majority support. The Presidency is strengthened with power to dissolve the National Assembly upon Presidential Decree.

Legislature under the 1999 Constitution

It is a unicameral legislature named as National Assembly. The Assembly is made up of 165 deputies, who are elected by universal, direct, personal and secret vote on a national party list proportional representation system. All deputies serve five year term and must appoint replacement to stand in for them in during periods of incapacity or absence (Article 186). They can be re-elected on upto two occasions. Deputies must be Venezuelan citizen by birth, or naturalized Venezuelans with a period of residency in excess of 15 years; older than 21 on the day of the election and have lived in the State for which they seek election during the previous four years. The first election of deputies to the new National Assembly took place on 30 July 2000.

Supreme Tribunal of Justice

Article 335 lays down that there shall be the supreme and ultimate interpreter of the Constitution and shall see to the uniform interpretation and application of the same. Interpretations established by the Constitutional Division concerning the contents or scope of Constitutional rules and principles are binding all of the courts of the Republic.

Article 336 empowers Supreme Tribunal of justice—(1) To declare the nullity, in whole or in part, of national laws and other acts of National Assembly with the force of law. (2) To declare the nullity, in whole or in part, of State Constitutes and laws, municipal ordinances and other acts of the deliberating bodies of the States or Municipalities which are issued by way of direct and immediate implementation of the Constitution and are in conflict with the same. (3) To declare the nullity, in whole or in part, of acts of National Executive which are in conflict with the Constitution. It is also to review the Constitutionality of decree of the President.

Amendment procedure

The Venezuelan Constitution provides a rigid procedure for bringing about amendment in any of its provisions. It prohibits any amendment which can erode or alter the fundamental structure of the Constitution. Whatever amendment is to be enacted, it must be in commensuration with the fundamental feature of the Constitution which includes its democratic set up based on separation of powers among 5 organs of government. Article 340 of the Constitution provides that the purpose of an amendment must be to add or to modify one or more articles of the Constitution, without altering the fundamental structure of the same. Article 341 provides the procedure for bringing about the amendments which shall be as follows:

(i) The initiative may emanate from 15% of the citizens registered with the civil and electoral registry, from 39% of the members of the National Assembly or from the President of the Republic.

(ii) When the initiative emanates from the National Assembly, the amendment shall require approval by a majority of the members of that body and shall be debated in accordance with the procedure established for the enactment of laws.

(iii) Electoral power shall submit the amendments to a referendum within 30 days of formally receiving the same.

(iv) Amendments shall be numbered consecutively and shall be published beneath the Constitution without altering the text of the latter, but with an annotation at the bottom of the amended article(s) of the number and date of the amendment modifying the same.

Article 344 provides for referring the amendment to a referendum within 30 days from its approval. The referendum shall pass on the reform as a whole, but up to one-third of the same may be voted on separately, if at least one-third of the National Assembly so agrees, or if in the initiative for the reform, the President of the Republic or a number of registered voters equivalent to at least 5% of the total registered with the Civil and Electoral Registry so requests.

POSITION UNDER INDIA CONSTITUTION

In comparison to the Constitutions of countries setting up Presidential form of Governments, the Indian Constitution presents a case of flexibility in amendment procedure. In a short span of 60 years of its working, it has been amended 112 times till year 2010. No other provision of the Constitution has acquired such controversial overtones as the provisions relating to the procedure of amendment as envisaged under Article 368. In the words of renowned jurist N.A. Palkhivala, it has been 'defaced' and 'defiled' in the guise of amendments. It has been subjected to frequent amendments and very often to suit political expediency and to counteract the decision of the Apex Court of the country which were deemed to be adverse leading to discomfiture.

Article 368 lays down the procedure for amendment under which the proposal to amend the constitution may be initiated only by the introduction of a Bill for the purpose in either House of Parliament and when the Bill is passed in each House by a majority of the total membership of that House and by a majority of not less than two-thirds of the members of that House present and voting, it shall be presented to the President who shall give his assent to the Bill and thereupon the Constitution shall stand amended in accordance with the terms of the Bill.

Provided that if such amendment seeks to make any change in:

(a) Article 54 (Election of President)

Article 55 (Manner of election of President)

Article 73 (the extent of executive power of the Union)

Article 162 (the extent of executive power of a State)

Article 241 (the setting up of a High Court in a Union Territory)

(b) Chapter IV of Part V (Provisions dealing with the Union judiciary)

Chapter V of Part VI (Provisions dealing with Courts in the States)

Chapter I of Part XI (Distribution of legislative powers)

(c) Any of the lists in the Seventh Schedule (Union, State and Concurrent list)

(d) The representation of States in Parliament or

(e) The provisions of this Article.

The amendment shall also require to be ratified by the legislatures of not less than one half of the States by resolutions to that effect passed by those legislatures before the Bill making provisions for such amendment is presented to the President for assent.

Nothing in Article 13 shall apply to any amendment under this Article. Thus Article 368 of the Constitution provides three-tier system of carrying out amendments. In the first category, amendments can be affected by a majority, such as required for the passing of an ordinary law. The amendments contemplated in Articles 4, 169 and 239A fall within this category and they are specifically excluded from the purview of the procedure prescribed in Article 368.

Second category covers those provisions which can be amended by a special majority of not less than two-thirds of the members of that House present and voting.

Third category refers to provisions listed out from (a) to (e) above which can be amended by special majority followed by ratification by resolutions passed by not less than one-half of the state legislatures.

The question whether power to amend Constitution extends to include fundamental rights also and whether amendment falls within the sweep of Article 13 of the Constitution has engaged a vociferous debate involving Supreme Court as well as Parliament. The judgment given in *Shankari Prasad* vs. *State of Rajasthan AIR 1959 SC 458*, *Sajjan Singh* vs. *State of Rajasthan AIR 1965 SC 845 (1965)*, *Golak Nath* vs. *State of Punjab AIR 1967 SCI 643* and *Kesavanand Bharti* vs. *State of Kerala AIR 1973(4) SCC 225* reflect how serious magnitude this subject had acquired. Article 13(2) says—"The State shall not make any law which takes away or abridges the rights conferred by this part and any law made in contravention of this clause shall, to the extent of the contravention, be void." The word law brings in its fold notification, rules, regulations, ordinance and any order having force of implementation. The question whether amendment to the Constitution is a law received serious contemplations from Supreme Court which initially held that amendment to the Constitution is entirely different from law. Since Constitution holds a special significance and acquires a distinct place than any law, an amendment to the constitution is equally different from the law. Constitutional law is the fundamental, superior or paramount law. Its authority and sanctions are higher than those of ordinary law. However, this view was overruled in landmark judgment pronounced in the case of *Golak Nath* vs. *AIR 1967 SC 1643* in which Supreme Court held that the word 'law' in Article 13(2) would not only cover a legislative measure but also a constituent measure so that Parliament had no power under Article 368 to make any law taking away or abridging any of the fundamental rights under Part III of the Constitution. This judgment drew its strength.

PARLIAMENTARY SYSTEM—NOT A BASIC STRUCTURE OF THE CONSTITUTION

Parliamentary system of government has never been regarded as Basic Structure of the Constitution though it remained a subject of fiery debate in the Constituent Assembly and later also in the Supreme Court. Shri B.N. Rau who played a significant role in drafting the constitution himself revealed in his speech before first batch of IAS probationers in June 1948 that there was a fairly strong current of feeling in favour of the American Presidential system and this found expression in certain decision of the Assembly. Mr. M.C. Chhagla, member of the Constituent Assembly had vehemently opposed Parliamentary form of government. The question whether parliamentary system of government forms part of the basic structure of the Constitution debated before Supreme Court in *Kesavanand Bharti* vs. *State of Kerala AIR 1973 1461.* It had ruled that Parliament derives its power to amend Constitution from the Constitution itself but such a power can not be exercised in such a manner so as to abrogate or emasculate the Constitution itself. There are basic structures contained in it which are outside the sweep of Parliament's powers and these include (i) Supremacy of the Constitution, (ii) Republican and Democratic form of Government, (iii) Secular character of the Constitution, (iv) Separation of powers between the legislature, the executive and the judiciary, and (v) Federal character of the Constitution. While Supreme Court included Separation of powers as basic structure, it refrained from including parliamentary system within the broad sweep of basic structures of the constitution. It even held that if our Parliamentary system was changed to a Presidential system, such a change is permissible under Article 368. Whether people would adopt such an amendment is a different matter and does not fall for consideration here. The core of the federal form of Government in our country is greater power in the Union Parliament than States for preserving the sovereignty of the country. To find out essential or non-essential features is an exercise in imponderables.

The debate over efficacy of parliamentary system of government acquired new dimensions when leaders, constitutional experts and even army chiefs join the chorus in expressing their voice of dissent. General K.M. Cariappa, P.P. Kumarmangalam, K. Subba Rao, P.B. Gajendragadkar, M. Hidayatullah and Vasant Sathe expressed their frustration and disgust with Indian political scene and asserted that if a polarization of political forces did not take place and the large number of parties did not integrate into two or three major ones, the parliamentary institutions might not survive, and even if they did they would not be effective.

Parliamentary system came under sharp criticism from no less a person than Lok Sabha Speaker himself. Addressing a Conference of Presiding Officers of the State Legislatures on December 30, 1970, Lok Sabha Speaker G.S. Dhillon expressed his deep anguish over the gathering storm and warned that these do not augur well for the future of democracy and the parliamentary system in India (December 31, 1970). Going a step further and seeing the decline, if not the demise of parliamentary institutions, Dharam Vira, former Governor, observed that it was not the Westminster type of parliamentary government that had failed in India but it was the people who had failed the parliamentary form of government. Jayaprakash Narayan, Neelam Sanjiva Reddy and B.K. Nehru also stated in unambiguous terms that the country was not fit for parliamentary system of government of Westminster type and that it should be replaced by a Presidential form of government. They had argued that switching over to Presidential form of Government will promote greater degree of stability as survival of the Executive would no longer depend upon the numerical strength of house. The ugly trends of horse-trading to buy or sell legislators which make the democratic process as ridiculous would come to an end. It will go to put an end to corruption as MPs/MLAs would no longer lobby to become ministers. Once an Executive becomes answerable to people, there can not be a vote bank politics as a candidate has to make an appeal to whole of the country and not to one segment or constituency comprising a particular section of the society. It will effectively put an end to the politics of defection, politics of regionalism and politics of lobbyism. For a candidate who would be seeking mandate from the whole of electorate on all India basis, it would be entirely difficult rather impossible to make a sectarian or communal appeal as he has to enlist the support of all segments of society taken together. Voters too have to vote a person from his overall standing performance and past conduct in totality. Exponents of parliamentary form of government who opposed switching over to Presidential form of government are those who are getting maximum advantages from it in terms of getting executive powers and passing on berths like legacy for their progeny. Presidential form of government is indeed democratic includes basic structure of the Constitution as referred to by the Supreme Court while delivering historic verdict in Kesavananda Bharati case. It is not going to erode federal system and separation of powers which are primordial rights and freedom of the people which together constitute basic structure of the constitution.

While presenting "National Government Agenda for new India", Vasant Sathe remarked: "It must be remembered that parliamentary democracies, as they are broadly called, are essentially party oriented systems of working of governments. Although Constitution like that of India makes no mention of political parties and theoretically Parliament consists only of individual representatives elected from their constituencies for the stipulated period, it was always envisaged that elections would be held on the basis of political parties." While the essence of democracy lies in the expression of people's will as ultimate goal, the system of government whether Parliamentary or Presidential are the means through which this goal can be achieved. Therefore, it is not the mode of governance or form of government which is the basic structure but the expression of people's will through democratic means which constitutes the corner-stone of the constitution. Institutions like Parliament are the creatures of the Constitution and derive strength and sustenance from it. They are subservient to the supremacy of the Constitution. An institution such as

Parliament which is an offspring of Constitution can not be termed as basic structure of the Constitution. It is to assist in achieving goals as enshrined in the preamble to the Constitution.

The essential attribute of a parliamentary system is accountability of executive before Parliament, Parliament's power to remove the executive, executive being part of the parliament and ministers are bound to be the members of parliament, collective responsibility of entire cabinet with prime minister as primus inter pares. Another attribute of parliamentary system is the ceremonial supremacy of the King or Head of the State. Parliament is supreme and possesses all powers and can pass any law and adopt any resolution or issue orders through government except to make a man a woman or woman a man. Such a system was unfamiliar to India as we never had the same grounds with same culture representing two-party system and strong parliamentary conventions. Constitutional reforms beginning from 1909 to 1919 and from 1935 to 1947 led this system to develop roots on Indian soil. It picked up gradually taking a zig-zag course reflected in formation and collapse of provincial governments under Government of India Act 1935. Nevertheless, framers of the Constitution acquired familiarity with the Parliamentary system and they could not resist it even though majority of these were speculative about its success. They just copied it *mutatis mutandis* without drawing a comparison between the economic and political contours of the two countries. While India is a big country called sub-continent, has a heterogeneous group of people having diverse culture, religion and social moorings, Britain is not. While India is a federal State, Britain is not. While India has more than 750 political parties, Britain has two party system. While British respects and follows conventions and precedents, we on the other hand, go against conventions and precedents. There is total lack of similarity between the two countries. It is like East is East, West is West and never the Twain shall meet. The Parliamentary system based on Westminster model of Britain was therefore not the right prescription to heal the age-old wounds afflicting the nation and the people. If it was accepted, it was in the hope that it will in the gradual process provide succour to the teeming millions of our country. It was regarded as a "mechanism" to take this country to a higher pedestal. Hence there is no cogent ground to regard the Parliamentary system as basic structure of the Constitution.

N.A. Palkivala, a renowned jurist, in his book *Our Constitution-Defaced and Defiled* writes that there can not possibly be any mistake about the authentic voice of our Constitution, its ringing tones proclaiming the sanctity of our sovereign democratic republic and the rights and duties of freedom. The Preamble to our Constitution, which is regarded as "key to open the mind of the makers" does not lay any focus on the form of government but only on the ideals like justice, social, economic, equality, liberty and fraternity besides declaring India as Sovereign, Democratic Republic States. Though Preamble is both introductory and declaratory in nature, no amendment of the Constitution, which is inconsistent with the Preamble, can be made. Supreme Court in *Berubari Case (1960) 3SC R 250 AIR 1960 SC 845* held that Preamble is not a part of the Constitution. Yet it is to act as an implied limitation on the power of amendment. It is not a source of any substantive powers because such powers are expressly granted in the body of the Constitution. The solemnity and dignity attached to the Preamble appears to be an epitome of the basic features of the Constitution. Though no esoteric test can be laid down to discern the essential features of our Constitution, yet he has laid down some of the essential features of the Constitution which are sacrosanct and Parliament can not alter or destroy in the exercise of its amending power. He has tried to list such basic structure as follows:

(i) The Supremacy of the Constitution. Ours is a "controlled constitution" par excellence. All institutions, including Parliament, are merely creatures of the Constitution and none of them is its master.

(ii) The sovereignty of India. The country can not be made a satellite, colony or dependency of any foreign country.

(iii) The integrity of the country. The unity of the nation, transcending all the regional, linguistic, religious and other diversities, is the bed-rock on which the Constitutional fabric has been raised.

(iv) The republican form of government. India can not be transformed into a monarchy.

(v) The democratic way of life as distinct from mere adult franchise. There is a guarantee of fundamental rights to ensure justice, social, economic and political; liberty of thought, expression belief, faith and worship, and equality of status and of opportunity.

(vi) A state in which there is no state religion. All religions are equal and none is favoured.

(vii) A free and independent judiciary. Without it, all rights would be writ in water.

(viii) The dual structure of the Union and the States. It permits centralization and decentralization to co-exist.

(ix) The balance between the legislative, the executive and the judiciary. None of the three organ can use its powers to destiny the powers of the other two, nor can any of them abdicate its power in favour of another.

(x) The amendability of the Constitution according to the basic scheme of Article 368. The constitution must continue to be amendable without being alterable in its essentials.

As Parliament like any other institutions is an organ of the political system under the Constitution, it derives its strength from the Constitution and remains subservient to its paramountcy. To search for an alternative or to switch over to American Presidential system of government would be an exercise in imponderables for the simple reason that those who are thriving on the parliamentary system currently in vogue, would never like to lose this goldmine which is a source of their survival.

15

Constitutional Provisions which would Require Revision for Switching over to Presidential System

A transition from Parliamentary system to Presidential system would entail amendments in the following articles of the Constitution for which Parliament is competent to do so as brought from the substance of the Supreme Court's decision in Kesavananda Bharti's case.

Article 53(3) (a) and (b): The article states that "nothing shall be deemed to transfer to the President any functions conferred by any existing law on the Government of any State or other authority; or (b) prevent Parliament from conferring by law functions on authorities other than the President." These would have to be repealed and to be substituted with words—"The President shall be the head of the State and all executive powers concerning the Union shall be vested in him." Several other powers vested in the President will continue so as to include power to grant pardon and remit punishments, important appointments including appointment of Governors, judges of the Supreme Court and High Courts, Chairman and members of the Public Service Commission, the Attorney General, the Chief Election Commissioner, and the Comptroller and Auditor General of India. He appoints the Election and Finance Commission and other commissions which would report on the administration of the scheduled area. Wide powers are given to the President in an Emergency including the power to suspend the enforcement of fundamental rights. The legislative power extends to the issuing of ordinance during the recess of Parliament. Every Bill to become law requires his assent. He can refuse his assent to a Bill or send it back for reconsideration. State laws relating to certain matters are not to be effective unless assented to by the President. But these powers are subject to provisions contained in Articles 74 and 75 which say that there shall be a Council of Ministers to aid and advise the President in the exercise of Ministers his functions. Article 75(3) lays down that the Council of and such a body must have a constitutional status in the absence of which it would be difficult for the President to discharge his duties as executive head of the State.

Article 61—Procedure for impeachment of the President. This provision will require to be amended to incorporate the same method as prevalent in countries practising Presidential system of government.

Article 73—Provision under this article shall have to be modified as the powers of the President would no longer be subjected to the legislature for the matters which fall within the domain of executive powers only.

Articles 74, 75—Council of Ministers to aid and advise President. The entire provision under these Articles shall have to be repealed as President shall no longer be dependent upon the Council of Ministers as there shall be no such Council as main task of legislature shall be to legislate on matters falling within its jurisdiction and list of powers. There shall be no such doctrine of 'collective responsibility of executive before Parliament' under the Presidential system.

Article 78—Duties of Prime Minister. As the Presidential system does not envisage the existence of Prime Minister or council of minister, this article shall have to be repealed.

Article 79—Constitution of Parliament. The words—"there shall be a Parliament for the Union" shall be repealed as instead of Parliament, provision for a union bicameral legislature can be considered to be added on the pattern as prevalent in United States.

Article 80—Composition of the Council of States. While the provision for such a Council of States may continue with provisions to model it on the pattern of Senate, its scope of powers, manner of representation may be amended.

Article 81—Composition of the House of People—Provision with regard to House of People and its composition may continue because it is not the existence of House which is subject matter but the powers it enjoys over executive and the doctrine of 'collective responsibility of executive before parliament' that form subject matter for any repealing exercise.

Articles 83, 84, 85 and 86—Which pertain to duration of Houses of Parliament, session of Parliament, prorogation and dissolution of Parliament, and right of President to address and send messages to Houses may require suitable modifications.

Article 123—President's power to promulgate Ordinance during recess of Parliament has to be amended to ensure that there shall not be a breach of doctrine of separation of powers while exercising such power of issuing Ordinance.

Article 368—This article provides for power of Parliament to amend the Constitution and procedure therefore. So long as the union legislature enjoys such a power, it would be difficult for Presidential system to set its foot and survive in the given political situation. By virtue of such powers, Union Legislature would be able to curtail the executive powers of President and may also breach the doctrine of separation of powers with checks and balances. In USA, amendment of the Constitution may be proposed only by Congress, with the approval of two-thirds of majority of both Houses or a convention summoned on an application from two-thirds of the members of both Houses. The proposed amendments must subsequently be ratified by at least three-fourths of the total number of the State legislatures or by convention in three-fourths of the total number of the States. It would therefore be imperative that such a rigid procedure of amendment be introduced to make it absolutely beyond purview of any of organ of government to encroach upon the power or jurisdiction of another organ.

A question was raised before Supreme Court in Kesavananda case as to whether Parliament, under Article 368, rewrite the entire Constitution and bring in a new Constitution? The answer to the question as given by the apex court is that Parliament can only do that which does not modify the basic features of the Constitution and not go beyond that. In *Minerva Mills Ltd.* vs. *Union of India*, the scope and extent of the doctrine of basic structure was again considered by the Supreme Court. The Court again reiterated the doctrine that under Article 368, Parliament can not so amend the Constitution as to damage the basic or essential features of the Constitution and destroy its basic structure. In *Kihoto Hollohon AIR 1993 SC 412,* Supreme Court declared: "Democracy is the basic feature of the Constitution and the Rule of law are part of it." It is not the form of government but the manner in which government is formed which is essential. Whether a feature of the Constitution is 'basic' or not is to be determined from time to time by the court as and when the question arises. The amendments as discussed hereinbefore lead us to a broad assessment in the event of their incorporation, the basic structure of the Constitution would remain intact. While judiciary already enjoys independence with power of judicial review, it may not entail as much amendments as required in the case of Union Executive and Union Legislature. Regarding working of similar system in States, regional aspirations will have to take due care and whatever amendments are proposed in the case of arrangements in States, it may depend upon the working of Presidential system at the Centre level. In any case, it is a marathon exercise for which a broad consensus amongst different sections of society, political parties and organizations. A Constitution Review Committee comprising non-political legal experts with long standing in their career needs to be constituted to take on such a matter and invite nation-wide debate.

Looking to the present political scenario there appears hardly any possibility to take even the first initiative in that direction. Every political party is in the grip of vested interests and national interests have taken back seat. They are unlikely to view the reforms keeping national interests in mind but shall go by the system which would be beneficial for their survival. In fact Parliamentary system provides a sort of Chess board where the politicians are at ease to indulge in lobbyism and play their dice more effectively to serve their political ends. Dynastic politics has come to stay and days are not far when assemblies would give a look of 'community hall'—a biggest ever joke on the so called 'largest democracy of the world'. Such a possibility appears to be dim in the case of Presidential system. Once the President shall be elected directly by the people without having to depend upon legislators to form a government, there can hardly be the practice of defection, horse-trading and other malpractices to pull down or form a government. Under such a system, there is no question of political leaders to remain busy in capturing ministerial berths either for themselves or for their progeny. They can have time to look after the problems being faced by the country and the people instead of indulging in lobbyism to somehow capture ministerial berths.

16

State Funding of Elections—Some Aspects

Increasing use of unaccounted money in elections and companies' donations to political parties have all along been considered as another factor leading to the decline of parliamentary system. It has caused acrimonious debates in and outside Parliament with experts demanding State Funding of elections as a panacea to salvage democratic system in the country. It amounts to political corruption, the fountainhead of all scams having its cascading effects on constitutional institutions like legislatures, bureaucracy, police, business and corrupting the entire polity. It was in 1995 when country witnessed an unprecedented furore when Harshad Mehta declared in public that he had paid Rs. 1 crore to the former Prime Minister P.V. Narasimha Rao as donation to the party for getting him off the hook. This un-ending sad commentary reached to the portals of Parliament when during the debate on No-confidence motion on 22nd July 2008, wads of currency notes for same amount were flaunted on the table of Lok Sabha with the allegation that the amount was paid to them for shifting loyalty in favour of ruling UPA combine. Whole country was flabbergasted to witness the hoary scenes of political corruption reaching to its lowest ebb. It remains no secret that there is a strong nexus between business houses and the political parties. In spite of numerous suggestions and recommendations of experts and the Committees, the corporate money power has been muddying the political process in the country since long. If a political party comes into power by depending upon the financial support of corporate sector, it will be well nigh impossible for it to resist the pressure for a *quid pro quo* from the companies. It is this unholy alliance between political parties and big companies which is casting its ugly shadow on the entire working of democratic system taking it to the brink of decline. It is ironical that every political party speaks against use of un-accounted money in elections but does nothing to curb it in any manner.

To curb the growing menace of money, the Government of India constituted a High Power Expert Committee in 1978 to review Companies Act 1956. It was presided over by a judge of Delhi High Court with members as top lawyers, industrial houses, trade union leaders and accountants. It unanimously recommended that the ban on political donations by companies to political parties should continue. The report laid emphasis on the ban and declared that the danger to the democracy can well be thwarted and freed from the clutches of large companies and business houses which dictate their terms in lieu of giving financial aid to the political parties. It is a sad commentary on the state of affairs that in spite of such a warning, Section 293A was amended in 1985 and Board of Directors was authorised to make donation to political parties. While other countries regard this unholy alliance as danger to democracy, we are still continuing with it. Now adding to this murky practice, the Government of India has allowed 100% tax deduction on companies and individuals contributing to electoral trusts. Such donations are created as pass-through vehicles for routing donations to political parties and are approved by the Central Board of Direct Taxes. It is envisaged that political parties may hope to get more donations now. This is contrary to what was recommended by the committees and experts in the field. In 2003, Government of India had enacted a law that made private donations to political parties easier. This law allows contributions by private companies to political parties with a maximum limit of 5% of their profits. It also makes it mandatory for contributions to be made by cheque and requires that parties audit their annual accounts and maintain a list of donors who give in excess of Rs. 20,000 and submit this to the Election Commission. But companies shy away from expressing affiliation to any particular political party by giving it direct donations. Courts in this country have been ruling against the donations from companies. Calcutta High Court once warned that its dangers are manifold. In the bid for political favouritism by the bait of money the company which will be the highest bidder may secure the most unfair advantage over the rival trader companies. It will mark the advent and entry of the voice of the big business in politics and in the political life of the country.

In June 1998, the Government of India constituted yet another Committee comprising members of all parliamentary parties under the chairmanship of Indrajit Gupta of the Communist Party of India (CPI) to look into the question of state funding of elections. The other members of the committee were Somnath Chatterjee of the CPI(M), Dr. Manmohan Singh of the Congress (I), Madhukar Sarpotdar of the Shiv Sena, Vijay Kumar Malhhotra of BJP, Sedapatti R. Muthiah of the All India Anna Dravida Munnetra Kazhagam (AIADMK) and Digvijay Singh of the Samata Party. After holding extensive discussions with political parties across the country, the committee prepared its report and submitted it to the Union Home and Law Ministries. It has recommended far-reaching measures to reform a key aspect of the electoral process, i.e. funding of political parties and candidates. The committee has made out a strong case for state funding of elections because political parties performed a vital public function to sustain democracy. However, it has recommended that such funding should be confined to parties recognised as national parties or State parties by the Election Commission and to candidates fielded by such parties.

Members of the Committee believed that the ideal situation was total state funding for elections. A broad consensus also emerged for partial funding in view of budgetary constraints and the prevailing economic conditions. The Committee indicated that the ultimate aim should be that all legitimate expenses of political parties are funded by the state. However, for the present it has recommended that the state should meet some essential expenses of political parties during election campaigns and provide them administrative support during the period of elections. It was viewed that political parties should be discouraged from seeking any external funding except a nominal membership fee to run their affairs, carry out political programmes and conduct election campaigns. The committee has laid emphasis on the need for greater insulation between political parties and private contributions of funds. As election campaigns require huge amounts of money and the costs of routine political activity between elections are also substantial, political parties have become overly dependent on private contributions, often acquired through questionable means and usually on the basis of a *quid pro quo*. Business houses and entrepreneurs contribute funds to political parties and seek to influence government decisions through them.

The state funding of political parties has been assailed on the ground that subsidies paid in the form of cash are likely to be misappropriated. The Committee therefore recommended that subsidies be extended to recognised political parties and their candidates in the form of facilities rather than in terms of cash. Thus every recognised national party may be allotted rent-free accommodation for its headquarters in New Delhi and every recognised State party may be provided the same facility in the respective state capitals. It recommended that the State may provide rent-free telephonic connection with subscriber trunk dialing facility. The Committee also endorsed the suggestion to direct Election Commission to allocate sufficient time free of cost on Doordarshan and All India Radio to recognised political parties for election broadcast and suggested that the facility be extended to private television channels in order to ensure fair and balanced coverage. It was also recommended that the state should provide every candidate of the recognised parties a specified quantity of petrol or diesel to run vehicles during an election campaign, a specified quantity of paper to prepare election literature and voter identity slips, postal stamps for a specified sum of money, five copies of the electoral roll in a constituency and an amplifier system for every Assembly constituency for every Assembly segment of a Lok Sabha constituency.

Realising the potential threat to democracy posed by the use of black money in elections, Law Commission of India also made several recommendations. In its 170th report on the Reform of the Electoral Laws, it recommended various measures to ensure electoral system free from malpractices and use of un-accounted money. The Commission reiterated its proposal to delete Explanation-1 to Section 77(1) of the Representation of Peoples Act 1951, which has been strongly criticised in several judgments of the Supreme Court. It recommended that political parties should maintain accounts as a mandatory requirement and get them audited for filing them before the Election Commission. On State funding of political parties, the Law Commission endorsed the recommendations of Indrajit Committee Report.

On December 23, 2005, the Union Cabinet approved in principle the law ministry's proposal for State Funding of elections. A Bill recommending state funding of elections was also referred to the Election Commission of India for its opinion. As per the proposal, candidates from recognised political parties will receive state funding. The Election Commission will be consulting different political parties on the issue before taking a final decision, sources said. However, Election Commission views the subject of state funding of elections in an entirely different manner. According to Election Commissioner S.Y. Quraishi, during his address at the seminar on electoral reforms, organised by Foundation for Advanced Management of Elections, said that Public funding of elections is not the solution. Who will give guarantee that it will stop the flow of black money. He, however, said that ceiling for spending in the elections can be increased from the present level of Rs 25 lakh per candidate in the Lok Sabha polls. He expressed the hope that ceiling of expenditure can be rationalised and ceiling level can be increased. Senior Advocate and BJP leader Arun Jaitley said that the real threat to the electoral process is coming from the money power.

An empirical study of state funding of elections as prevalent in different countries would enable us to reach to the conclusion that this practice has been successful in its prime object to decrease the dependence of political parties on companies for the need of financing elections. However, in India such a possibility of achieving success in its prime objective may not provide a fool-proof arrangement unless political parties themselves come forward to make this a success. It is precisely for this reason that remarks of S.Y. Quraishi that even state funding will not prevent or deter our political parties to cut the cakes with companies to remain in race for a high-voltage campaign.

In United Kingdom, elections are characterised by very short campaigns requiring modest expenditure. Candidates receive subsdies in the form of free postage for communication to each voter, free use of public halls for meetings and election broadcasts on radio and Television. Opposition parties also get small grants of about two to three million pounds from government for office expenses and not elections. In USA the candidates are required to disclose the sources of their funds and their accounts are examined by the Federal Election Commission. A unique feature of the American system is that in the Presidential elections, the federal government provides limited assistance to the candidates even for the pre-nomination campaign. The candidate must first himself raise $5000 with contributions of $250 or less in each of at least 20 states. The Federal government then makes a matching contributions upto $250 dollars for each contributions raised by the candidate. The federal government also provides public funds for party convention.

In Germany, a regular system of government grants to political parties is in force since 1959. The grant is DH 5 per vote polled by the party. Parties getting less than 0.5 per cent of the total votes are not eligible to receive any subsidy. The practice of state funding has had a healthy effect on the electoral process. Yet it is considered doubtful if this system will get success looking to the deceitful role played by different groups or parties in India.

In France also the candidates who secure at least 5 per cent votes get reimbursement of expenditure on certain items such as issue of notices and circulars subject to the maximum of Fr. 1,00,000. Public premises for holding meeting, etc. are made available free of charge. The manifesto of each candidate is printed and delivered to each voter by the State directly.

In Japan, political parties receive a subsidy of about $70,000 per member of Parliament. Donations to individual candidates are limited to $15,000. There is widespread political corruption mainly because of the large expenditure which MPs are required to incur on nursing their constituency. The use of posters and pamphlets is strictly regulated and candidates appear on the non-commercial public television station to give campaign speeches. Most of this activity is publicly funded. Likewise countries like Belgium and Canada have evolved their system of funding election spendings and no chinks or loopholes appeared in the working of system.

The entire gamut of State Funding requires broadly speaking nine variables which include (i) Recipients, (ii) Providers, (iii) Eligibility criteria, (iv) Level of funding, (v) Timing of payment, (vi) Spending restrictions, (vii) Reporting Obligations and Monitoring, (viii) Sanctions affecting subsidies, and (ix) Maintaining books of accounts. We may discuss these variables as follows:

State funding should not be discriminatory as otherwise it may attract legal scrutiny for violation of right to equality and equal protection of law. Yet, rules can be framed to discriminate between old political parties and new political parties. While the newly formed parties can be allowed to use indirect subsidies such as free broadcasting, etc. the old parties may get the subsidies based on their past standing and mass appeal and also in terms of their gains of seats and vote percentage during previous elections.

(i) **Recipients:** The first and foremost requirement in the exercise of state funding pertains to the task of identifying the political parties or the entities to whom the subsidies are to be extended. This requires lots of scrutiny on the basis of pre-drawn guidelines.

(ii) **Providers:** Subsidies can be provided by public bodies such as Ministries of Finance, public undertakings, municipal bodies or any specific organisation which may be entrusted with the task of maintaining special fund for this purpose. A committee of reputed impartial persons can be set up to decide the quantum of subsidies and the source through which it is to be augmented.

(iii) **Eligibility criteria:** The threshold of eligibility criteria can be based on the amount of private money collected by a party, the number of members registered in the party, the number of votes received in certain election, or the number of seats they hold in the national or local assemblies. Compliance with the disclosure and other guidelines without breach may be the other criteria. A party or person can be disqualified to be eligible in the event of violation of any rule or guideline in this regard.

(iv) **Level of funding:** The levels of direct public funding in transition stages differ considerably. The amount appropriated could either be an amount fixed by law or per capita per voter.

(v) **Timing of payment:** Subsidies can be provided on annual, quarterly or monthly basis, before or after elections. There should be a clear deadline for the distribution of the grants. These deadlines will allow the political parties to engage in proper budgeting. Further, periodic distribution of public funds can allow time to audit financial statements before further distribution for the year. This adds teethes to the promise to withhold funds if full public disclosure has not been made or if a party has committed serious violations.

(vi) **Spending restrictions:** There are distinctions between countries regarding the purposes for what the public subsidies may be used.

(vii) **Reporting obligations and monitoring:** A growing number of countries require political entities to disclose publicly that subsidies have been spent transparently and according to rules.

(viii) **Sanctions affecting subsidies:** One of the most effective ways to secure compliance with different political finance regulations is to limit or withdraw public funding from parties and candidates that do not take their obligations seriously.

17

Compulsory Voting— Its Feasibility and Implications

Several fast emerging ominous trends in our electoral system to settle down as permanent features relate to voters' apathy towards exercise of their franchise. In fact voters' turn out has been decreasing in modern democracies. As high turn out is considered to be a desirable condition for any democratic system, the decline can be perceived as threat to democracy. Decisions made by government are more legitimate when higher proportion of population participate and casting vote is the best way to enable people to participate in the democratic process. Another reason in support of heavy voters turn out is that it reduces the financial burden on the political parties and candidate who have to incur heavy expenditure to make people come out to cast their votes. The solution therefore lies in introducing compulsory voting as that would reduce the election expenses which in turn reduce the dependence of political parties on big business houses for seeking finance resulting in a healthy, vibrant and resurgent democratic system. It will also help the Governments to reduce their expenditure on highly expensive advertisements through hoardings, newspapers and other means of communication like radio and television asking people to vote.

The opponents of compulsory voting, however, argue that it is wholly arbitrary and asking the voters to vote as a mandatory requirement against their will is undemocratic by its very nature. They argue that non-voting *en masse* is sometimes resorted to by villagers as a measure of protest. If such people are forced to cast votes against their will, it will be an attempt to muzzle their right of protest. But these arguments hold no sound proposition because compulsory voting has a provision for casting a blank vote also. If a voter does not want to cast his vote in favour of any candidate, he has the option to cast his vote as blank. But in any case, non-voting can not be regarded as a better measure of lodging protests against government or district administration. Such non-voting will hardly result in creating any pressure on the departments. It is rather voting *en-masse* against the candidates supporting such departments which may be a comparatively better option rather than non-voting. Moreover, compulsory voting does not mean that a non-voter can be regarded as an offender. The maximum penalty that has ever been applied is the fine of some paltry amount and even that may also be ignored if the voter is able to lead sufficient cause for not being able to cast his vote due to the reason of either his sickness, old age, outside the country or involved in some compulsive circumstances for which he shall be at liberty. In fact, arguments against introduction of compulsory votings are less and limited than the arguments for its introduction. If we weigh both the arguments and try to put them to test on the basis of empirical analysis, it would not be difficult to conclude that the compulsory voting has the better ground to prevail. This is also strengthened by the fact that in all countries wherein this system is prevalent, the political fall outs have been far better and have virtually led to the emergence of healthy and vibrant political trends.

To strike a balance between exponents and opponents of compulsory votings, some measures may be suggested in the form of INCENTIVE VOTING! In that case the grievance of opponents would be fully met with. Such incentive measures can be introduced in a manner without causing any expenditure at all. Currently, the Election I Cards do not carry any validity period which is a must in case of any other Identity Card. It is this indefinite period of Election I Card which is another factor needs to be addressed to. I suggest that after every five years or General Election whichever comes earlier, the Election Identity Cards must be renewed for another five year term. This can be done at the Polling Booth itself. When a voter will realize that his Election Identity Card is also being renewed simultaneously on the day of polling, he would be prompted to visit polling booth to cast his vote at the same lime. Such a system can be experimented in any municipality election to assess and examine its viability for extending it to other parts of the country. This system of incentive voting can go to a greater extent of striking a balance between two extremes.

The substantial fall in voters' turn out in every successive election has virtually posed a question mark on the efficacy of the entire expensive exercise. Election Identity Cards with their indefinite validity period are being used more as ID proof than for casting votes. If this trend continues to persist, our claim of having largest democracy would become as tall as largest number of people not exercising franchise. Recently in Australia 94.3% voters turned out to cast votes. If we compare this to our system, we are lagging far behind and even 50 per cent turn out is considered heavy. There are about 32 countries in the world wherein system of compulsory voting is working smoothly.

Compulsory voting is not a new concept. Countries which introduced this system include nearly 32 countries. An empirical study of the working of compulsory voting in these countries would reveal that the system is working well without any bottlenecks except that it may not be liked by regional or linguistic pressure groups whose interests are better met when voters belonging to their ideologies alone cast the votes. The first ever country which introduced compulsory voting was Belgium which made it a mandatory requirement by law in 1892 for every voter to cast its vote. Then it was Argentina which introduced this system in 1914. Then Australia which introduced it in 1924. The other countries wherein this system is currently in vogue include Georgia, Austria, Netherland, Venezuela, Brazil, Chile, Singapore, Turkey, Uruguay and Democratic Republic of Congo, etc. In Bolivia, if a voter fails to participate in an election, the citizen may be denied withdrawal of his or her salary from the Bank for three months. In Turkey, according to a law passed by Parliament in 1986, if an eligible elector does not cast a vote he or she has to pay a fee of 5 YII (3 US Dollar). The exponents of compulsory voters argue that wherever it is in force, it has substantially reduced the financial burden on political parties to arrange for additional financial resources and thus their dependency on industrial houses has also decreased resulting in setting up a bondage-tree government without any arms-twisting by such financiers. It has also enabled the people to think constructively and apply their best reasoning to the country's political and financial affairs resulting in active participation of people. A democratically elected government is truly democratic only when it gets the largest chunk of peoples support reflected in the majority of votes it secures.

Voting facilities such as proxy voting, mail voting, two-day voting or e-votings are becoming more and more popular. In India, women voters comprise the major portion of non-voting population. Then comes the personnel from armed forces, police and employees deployed on election duty. Together, these alone constitute more than two crores voters. There is no reason why proxy voting, postal-balloting, or e-voting should not be introduced to enable such a huge chunk of population to exercise their right of franchise.

In India, it was the Chief Election Commissioner who took initiative in this direction when he wrote to the Government of India in 1963 recommending the introduction of compulsory voting in the country. Had his recommendation been conceded, much of the problems arising out of linquism, provincialism and heavy financial burden on political parties to bring voters at polling booths would have been solved. But such a recommendation was not even debated upon perhaps for the reason that it would have gone against the interest of ruling party which thrives on vote bank politics. Thus the ennobling recommendations by the Constitutional forum like Election Commission of India went un-heeded.

Realising the significance of compulsory voting, Gujarat Government became the first-ever state to introduce it by an act called "Gujarat Local Authorities Laws (Amendment) Bill 2009. Gujarat Assembly passed this Bill which shall have its impacts felt in municipal corporation elections going to poll in 2010. Surprisingly, the Congress(I) opposed the Bill vehemently. According to the Bill, if a voter fails to vote for reasons other than prescribed by the rules, he might be declared as a "defaulter voter" and face consequences, rules for which will be framed and placed before the assembly for approval later. The Bill makes voting in local body polls mandatory for the first time in the country. Immediately, thereafter, the Himachal Pradesh Chief Minister came out with announcement that his government too will introduce the Bill on similar lines so as to introduce the compulsory voting in his state. If this system came out successful in these two states, it is bound to be a precursor for the introduction of the same in the whole country. In fact a strong case has emerged for introduction of compulsory voting in the country. In this context this author would add here a copy of the letter addressed to the Chief Election Commission giving suggestions on introduction of compulsory voting as under:

GLV/Elec/2008 18-12-08

To

Hon'ble Chief Election Commissioner
Election Commission of India
Nirvachan Sadan
NEW DELHI

SUB:- SUGGESTIONS RELATING TO COMPULSORY VOTING

Respected Sir,

I would like to refer to several ominous trends in my electoral system which are fast emerging to settle down and cripple our polity. The substantial fall in voters' turn out in every successive election has virtually posed a question mark on the efficacy of the entire expensive exercise. Election Identity Cards with their indefinite validity period are being used more as ID proof than for casting votes. If this trend continues to persist, our claim of having largest democracy would become as tall as largest number of people not exercising franchise. Recently in Australia 94.3% voters turned out to cast votes. If we compare this to our system, we are lagging far behind and even 50 per cent turn out is considered heavy. There are about 32 countries in the world wherein system of compulsory voting is working smoothly. There is no dearth of data as honourable Commission might be aware of these aspects. We recall that once Election Commission itself had recommended for compulsory voting. In the changing scenario compulsory voting alone can work as panacea as it would reduce the electoral expenses of the candidates to a great extent in bringing out voters from their homes to take them to booths. In a fluid situation where fluctuation of just three or four per cent of votes result in change in formation of the government, compulsory voting would induce massive participation of people leading to a healthier democracy to be called the largest democracy in truest terms.

As the country is preparing for general election in early next year, we submit that in case measures to introduce compulsory voting can not be initiated for any technical reason, then Honourable Commission can at least consider "INCENTIVE VOTING" and we suggest following measures which are within its domain:

1. Presently, Election Identity cards are issued without any validity period. This is irrational as no identification card can be for an indefinite period of time. All other cards including D/L, etc. are subjected to renewal periodically. If the Election Commission prescribes a time limit for say five years and arranges for their renewal on the spot at the polling booth itself by embossing the card "Renewed for 5 years" or by taking fresh photograph for fresh card or by simply getting a form filled up at the polling booth itself for preparing the card later, it would definitely attract massive turn out of voters as it would be added with renewal of ID proof also. Such an exercise

would save lots of expenditure also because it would hardly require additional staff as the polling officer entrusted with the voter list can renew the card with an embossing equipment. It will also save the voters from visiting Election Office for getting the new cards prepared or renewal of the same. If the will to introduce reform is mustered, then various other steps can be considered by linking the Election Identity card to the actual exercise of voting.

2. Alternatively, a measure to issue fresh Identity Cards to those who cast their votes and invalidating all other cards of voters who do not cast votes can also be considered. Once a voter is aware that his card would loss its validity if he does not cast his vote, he would be prompted to visit Polling Booth on his own resulting in near hundred per cent polling. After all Election Cards are issued for Elections. "No vote no Card" policy can be considered. A public notice to this effect would be enough to send the voters to queue up at the polling booth to cast votes.
3. Another measure to ensure heavy polling can be issuance of a slip for having cast the vote on the spot at polling booth with same photo as in voters list and such a slip may be considered valid for latest ID proof and voter can get the same laminated for its safe preservation.
4. A large number of voters change their residences but their cards continue to show the old addresses. Issuance of a slip showing the latest address on some identification on the spot can also be considered to attract voters at the polling booths.
5. It is estimated that more than one crore officials including security personnel are deployed for conducting polls throughout the country. If army personnel deployed at strategic points and staff on deputation are included, the figure may swell further. They are deprived of casting their votes as the procedure for issuing ballot paper is too cumbersome

and the same is not provided in actual practice or simply discouraged deliberately. Depriving such a huge number of more than one crore voters their right to vote has perhaps escaped attention and may not stand the judicial scrutiny. You will appreciate that where victory margin is nominal, such votes can tilt the balance and change the colours of victory processions. There is no reason why compulsory voting can not start from such poll-related staff, if at all there is will to do so. We request that compulsory voting be introduced for all poll-related staff including personnel from security forces.

There are no dearth of data or idea. If there is any dearth it is that of will. We hope Election Commission would definitely consider above suggestions in the interest of our polity—the largest democracy which is converting into largest anarchy.

Thanking you,

(G.L. VERMA)

References

Besides consulting Constituent Assembly Debates, material available at Election Commission of India, several books, Supreme Court judgments, AIRs, journals Study papers, research works were also consulted apart from vast newspapers clippings.

1. *Constituent Assembly Debates.* (Nehru Museum Library)
2. *General Elections in India* by M.L. Ahuja.
3. *History of Parliament of India* by Dr. Subhash C. Kashyap.
4. "The Constitution and the Parliament in India" by S.L. Shakdhar.
5. *Indian Parliament* by Ajay K. Mehra.
6. *American Presidents* by Marcus Cunliff.
7. *India Since Independence—from Preamble to the Present* by V.K.N. Menon.
8. *Glimpses of working of Parliament* by S.L. Shakdher.
9. *A Constitutional History of India* by S.L. Sikri.
10. *Constitution-Defaced and Defiled* by N.A. Palkivallah.
11. *Subverting the Constitution* by G.G. Mirchandani.
12. *Indira after Gandhi* by Ramchandra Guha.
13. *Cabinet Government* by Ivor Jennings.
14. *Indian Constitutional Law* by M.P. Jain.
15. *The Hindu* dated 25-11-2003.
16. *The Hindustan Times* dated 26-11-2003.

17. *The Hindu* dated 27-11-2003.
18. *The Economic Times* dated 27-11-2003.
19. *The Hindustan Times* dated 6-11-2005.
20. *The Hindustan Times* dated 14-12-2005.
21. *The Times of India* dated 23-12-2005.
22. *The Times of India* dated 24-12-2005.
23. *The Times of India* dated 5-9-2005.
24. Article of Arun Jaitley. *The Hindustan Times* 27-12-2005.
25. *Navbharat Times* dated 27-11-2005.
26. *The Times of India* dated 22-1-2006.
27. *Hindustan* (Hindi) dated 22-1-2006.
28. *The Times of India* dated 23-1-2006.
29. *The Times of India* dated 25-1-2006.
30. *The Hindustan Times* dated 26-1-2006.
31. *The Hindustan Times* dated 31-1-2006.
32. *The Times of India* dated 29-1-2006.
33. Article "Democracy Derailed" by Soli Sorabjee *The Hindustan Times* 3-2-2006.
34. *Political System in India* by Verinder Grover.
35. *The Hindustan Times*, 31-5-2006.
36. *The Times of India*, 8-6-2009.
37. *The Hindu*, 31-5-2009.
38. *The Hindustan Times*, 11-9-2007.
39. Shashi Tharoor's article "Its time to rethink parliamentary system" *The Times of India*, 16-12-2007.
40. R. Venkataraman Speech dated 16-10-1999 at India Int. Centre.
41. Yogendra Yadav's article "Making sense of the verdict" *The Hindu*, 18-5-09.
42. *The Times of India*, 22-7-09 "Switch to Presidential system".

43. *The Times of India*, 24-12-2009.
44. *The Times of India*, 20-2-2009.
45. *The Hindu*, 17-5-2009.
46. Vir Sanghvi's article "Family Matters" *The Hindustan Times*, 26-10-2009.
47. *The Hindustan Times*, 23-10-2009. "Dynasty Wins".
48. Ronojoy Sen's article "Why Dynasties Flourish" *The Times of India*, 16-9-2009.
49. *Political Corruption in India* by Surendranath Dwivedi and G.S. Bhargava.
50. *The Dynasty—A Political Biography of the Premier Ruling Family of Modern India* by S.S. Gill.
51. *After Nehru* by G.S. Bhargava.
52. *Electoral System in India* by Election Commission of India.
53. Article by Ramchandra Guha—"Political Parties As Family Firms" *The Times of India*, 1-12-2005.
54. Alok Tikku's article "India Whining: Dirt in Parliament" *The Hindustan Times*, 20-1-2006.
55. *MPLAD—Concept, Confusion, Contradiction* by Era Sezhian MP.
56. "Another Sting: 7 MPs caught on camera." *Times of India*, 20-12-2005.
57. MPLADs funds to build quash courts in posh club.
58. *Hindustan* (Hindi) 22-6-2006.
59. *Two swords in one scabbard* by Vasant Sathe.
60. Letter dated 18-12-2008 to Chief Election Commissioner by Sh. G.L. Verma containing suggestions relating to compulsory voting.
61. Letter dated 10-01-2009 to Chief Election Commissioner by Sh S.K. Agarwal President Apex Society of Legal Awareness for compulsory voting and E-voting.

62. Letter dated 15-1-2009 of Shri S.Y. Qureshi, Election Commissioner to Shri S.K. Agarwal President of Apex Society Legal Awareness.

63. *The Times of India*, 1-12-2009—Question Hour collapses.

64. *The Times of India*, 5-12-2009 "Some MPs too busy for House panels".

65. Report of National Commission to Review the Working of the Constitution.

66. *The Times of India*, 22-10-2008 Outsource Parliament.

67. *The Times of India*, 21-10-2008 Parliament met for just 32 days.

68. *The Times of India*, 22-1-2007 Constitutional Dustbin.

69. *The Times of India*, 24-2-2008 "Presidential system promotes nationalism" An Article written by Shashi Tharoor.

70. *The Times of India*, 7-1-2010 "MPs House attendance hits new low".

71. Rajmohan Gandhi's book—"Sardar".